ABSTRACTS

OF

WILLS, INVENTORIES & ACCOUNTS

PATRICK COUNTY, VIRGINIA

1791 - 1823

By:
Lela C. Adams

Southern Historical Press, Inc.
Greenville, South Carolina

Copyright 1983
By: Lela C. Adams

Copyright Transferred 1984
By: Southern Historical Press, Inc.

All rights reserved. No part of this publication may be reproduced, stored in a retrieval system, transmitted in any form, posted on to the web in any form or by any means without the prior written permission of the publisher.

Please direct all correspondence and orders to:

www.southernhistoricalpress.com
or
**SOUTHERN HISTORICAL PRESS, Inc.
PO BOX 1267
375 West Broad Street
Greenville, SC 29601
southernhistoricalpress@gmail.com**

ISBN #0-89308-356-9

Printed in the United States of America

Will Book I pg 1   Date: 22 June 1790
Will of John Small of Henry County, Virginia.
Legatees: to my beloved wife, estate and moveables
during her natural life, then to the children to
wit: Matthew Small, Eggans Robson, Marthu Meeks,
Malen, Becky Mary Gem Hadcock, Sally Barnet, Esther
Denny. (no commas in document.)
Executors: Francis Turner, Thomas Morrey, James
Denny and Matthew Small.
Witness: William McPeak, Joseph Aleb.., James Denny.
Returned: August Court 1791

Will Book I pg 2   Date: 1791
Inventory of the estate of John Small, deceased.
Estate includes: pots, dishes, furniture, cattle
and one still valued at 63.6.8.
No total value
Appraisers: Francis Turner, Jeremiah Burnett, Sr.,
William McAlexander, Richard Pilson.

Will Book I pg 3   Date: 12 June 1792
Estate of Henry Parr, deceased. John Parr, Jr.
administrator.
An account of payments made:
20 Nov 1788 Note to Doctor Randleman
 6 May 1789 Paid William Carter
10 Jun 1789 Paid Benjamin Arnold, Palatiah Shelton
             and James Shelton
30 Jun 1789 Paid taxes to Sheriff
10 Nov 1789 to John Parr Sr, Samuel Sharp, William
             Fain and John Parr.
Items sold 8 April 1788
Purchasers: Arthur Parr, William Halbert, Peter Corn,
John Bottetourt, William Keaton, John Parr Sr, Z.
Keaton, James Scurlock, Abraham Eads, Hamon Critz,
Humberston Lyon, Mary Parr, Stephen Lyon, Milly Parr,
George Corn, James Bailey and Abraham Frazer.
Total: 57.19.9
Signed: Samuel Clark, William Banks, Stephen Lyon.

Will Book I pg 4   Date: 22 Aug 1793
Inventory of the estate of John Lackey, deceased.
Household items and livestock.
Total: 32.5.3
Appraised by: John Koger, John Farrol, David Harbour.
Returned: October Court 1793

Will Book I pg 5   Date: 23 Dec 1793
Inventory of the estate of Bartlett Foley, deceased.
Farm equipment, livestock, 3 tracts of land containing 143 acres, 171 acres and 491 acres. Total of the inventory: 126.12.6
Returned: Dec Court by H. Smith, John Koger and John Ferrell.

Will Book I pg 6   Date: 10 Dec 1793
Administrator's Bond of Shadrack Going, Thomas Ward and Joshua Adams. Shadrack Going being the administrator of the estate of Nathan Going, deceased.
Returned: Dec Court 1793

Will Book I pg 7   Date: 28 Feb 1794
Administrator's bond of Archs. Hughes, Samuel Clark and Hamon Critz. A. Hughes the administrator of the estate of William Manning, deceased.
Returned: Feb Ct 1794

Will Book I pg 8   Date: 8 Aug 1794
Memoranddum of the value of the estate of Abraham Bird. Furniture, farm equipment and livestock.
Total: 40.0.2
Returned: Augt Ct 1794

Will Book I pg 9   Date: 25 Sept 1794
Administrator's bond of George Hairston and Charles Thomas. George Hairston being the administrator of the estate of John Henderson, deceased.
Returned: Sept Ct 1794

Will Book I pg 10   Dated: 27 Feb 1795
Administrator's bond of Barberry Foley, David Morgan, John Farrell, Mary Foley, Rachel Foley, Nelly Foley, Biddy Foley and Elizabeth Dewesse. Barberry(Barbary) Foley being the administratrix of the estate of Bartholomew Foley.
Returned: Feb Ct 1795

Will Book I pgs 11,12   Date: 22 Feb 1793
Will of Frederick Fulkerson, being very sick and weak.
Legatees: Dearly beloved wife Milly 7 slaves, cattle, sheep, at her death the estate to be divded amongst the four children.
Beloved son James to receive slaves, cattle and one fourth of all horses, one feather bed and furniture, blacksmith tools and my big Dutch Bible.
To my loving daughter, a feather bed and furniture and pewter.
To my beloved daughter Debby Thomas, 2 slaves, 2 feather beds and furniture, one fourth part of the cattle and one half of the pewter.
To my beloved daughter Mary Hill, 2 slaves, feather beds and furniture.
Witness: Charles Sutton and Henry Franse
Returned: May Court 1795

Administrators bond of Milly Fulkerson, James Fulkerson, Archelaus Hughes and Samuel Clark. Milly Fulkerson the widow and relect of Frederick Fulkerson deceased and James Fulkerson administrators of the estate.

Pg 13   Date: 21 July 1796
Will of Thomas Harbour, being in a very low state of health.
Legatees: Beloved wife Kesiah Harbour all possessions during her widowhood. Children: sara Harbour, David Harbour, Thomas Harbour, Nancy Harbour and Joshua Harbour. Money is to be laid out in land in some new country where land is good and provide wife with a place to live on it. There is 300 pounds in money which I give and bequeath to be equally divided between my five beloved children.
Executors: My brother David Harbour, Jesse Spurlock and Benjamin Turman.
Returned: Sept Ct 1796

Pg 14   Date: 23 Feb 1797
Administrators bond of Isham Craddock and Barnard M. Price. Isham Craddock the administrator of the estate of Samuel King, deceased.
Returned: Feb Ct 1797

Pg 15   Date: 27 Sept 1798
Item: Will of Isam Webb, weak in body....
Legatees: My beloved wife Ann the cattle, horses and hogs, all household furniture and the still during her lifetime.
My eldest son William to have my gun.
My younger son Isam to have the blacksmith tools and the still after his mothers decease and to pay four pounds each to the rest of the heirs.
My three daughters to receive two certain pieces of land known as the "saw pit tract" and "the mill seat tract" joining Spencer Talley survey.
Witness: Jeremiah Jadwin and Solomon Jadwin
Ann Webb widow and relect
Returned: Jan Ct 1799.

pg 16   Date 8 Aug 1791
Item: Administrator's Bond of Matthew Small, Thomas Morrow, James Denny, John Henderson and James Nowlin. Matthew Small, Thomas Morrow and James Denny the executors of the estate of John Small, deceased.
Returned: Aug Ct 1791

Pg 17   Date: 12 Aug 1793
Item: Administrator's Bond of Peter Saunders and George Hairston. Peter Saunders the administrator of the estate of John Lacky, deceased.
Returned: Aug Ct 1793

Pg 18   Date: 9 Dec 1793
Item: Administrator's Bond of Cornelius Deweese and David Morgan. Cornelius Deweese the administrator of the estate of Bartlett Foley, deceased.
Returned: Dec Ct 1793

Pg 19   Date: 7 March 1794

Item: Appraisal of the estate of Humberston Lyon, deceased. By: John Parr, John Fletcher and David Rogers. Includes: Still, furniture, cyphering books, Bible, Surveyor's instruments, pocket book and neck buckle.
Returned: March Ct 1794

Will Book I pg 20   Date: 17 April 1794
Item: Sale of Goods of Humberston Lyon.
William Smith, Jr. Administrator.
Items sold to: John Parr, Jr., Edward Tatum, Nathaniel Smith, Nancy Lyon, William Smith, Sr., Thomas Frazer, William Smith, Jr., Henry Smith, Joseph Willis, Jr., and Hezekiah Shelton.
Total: 40.13.10½
Returned: April Ct 1794

Pg 21   Date 27 Feb 1794
Item: Administrator's Bond of William Smith, James Lyon, Archelaus Hughes. William Smith being the administrator of the estate of Humberston Lyon, deceased.
Returned: Feb Ct 1794

Pg 22   Date 23 May 1794
Item: Appraisal estate of Nathan Goings, deceased.
Includes: 4 Notes amounting to 24.2.3, hammer, gun, and rasp. Total: 25.8.10.
Appraisers: Obadiah Hudson, John Rea and James Taylor.
Returned: May Ct 1794

Pg 23   Date: 1 Aug 1794
Item: Administrator's Bond of Samuel Kennon and Job Ross. Samuel Kennon the administrator of the estate of Abraham Byrd, deceased.
Returned: July Ct 1794.

Pg 24   Date: 28 Aug 1794
Item: Administrator's Bond of Humphrey Smith and Nathan Hall. Humphrey Smith the administrator of the estate of Cornelius Deweese.
Returned: Aug Ct 1794

Pg 25   Date: 2 Jan 1794
Will of Cornelius Deweese
All of the estate to be sold, deducting the wife's part.
Wife: Dawry Deweese. Money to be equally divided amongst the children: William Deweese, Bartley Deweese and Mary Deweese. The two boys to be put to trade at the discretion of the executor.
Executor: My beloved friend Humphrey Smith
Witness: Beverage Hughes, Barbary Foley, Senr., and Briget Foley.
Returned: May Ct 1794.

Pgs 26, 26a, 26b   Date: 10 Aug 1795
Inventory of the estate of Frederick Fulkerson.
Includes: 9 slaves, 7 horses, cattle, sheep, hoggs, furniture, waggons, tools, books and a Dutch Bible.
Total: 634.7.4.
Appraisers: Peter Scales, Isaac Adams, Will Gray and Jacob Critze.
Returned: Aug Ct 1795

Pg 27   Date: 27 Jan 1795
Item: Inventory of goods and chattels of Cornelius Deweese.
Includes: Furniture, livestock, spelling book, etc.
Total: 6.3.6.
Appraisers: John Burnett, Micajah Burnet and William Fuson.
Returned: May Ct 1796.

Pg 27   Date: 27 Jan 1796
Item: Account of the sale of goods of Cornelius Deweese.
Total: 5.12.11. H. Smith, administrator.

Pg 28   Date: 26 Jan 1797
Item: Administrator's Bond of Mary Hughes, John Hughes, Brett Stovall, Theophilus Lacy, Arch. Hughes, Jonathan Hanby, William Carter, Thomas Mitchell, William Lindsay, Gabriel Penn and Peter Scales.
Mary Hughes, John Hughes and Brett Stovall, administrators of the estate of A. Hughes, deceased.
Returned: Jan Ct 1797.

Pg 29   Date: 14 Aug 1795
Item: Inventory of the estate of John Smallman.
Includes: furniture, cattle, a gun. Total: 46.13.6.
Appraisers: George Reeves, Joseph Cummins and Richard Tucker Maynor.
Returned: Aug Ct 1797

Pgs 30, 30a, 30b   Date: 3 Jan 1798
Item: Will of Richard Tucker Maynor
Legatees: son, William Maynor 5 shillings. Daughter, Ruth Bryant 4 shillings. Son Tucker Maynor 5 shillings, daughter Mary Johnson several articles lent her when she married. Daughter Pressiller Maynor, a feather bed, furniture and 25 pounds Current money of Virginia.

Son Isaiah Maynor 5 shillings and land on Bowen's Creek.
Son John Maynor, all my wearing clothes.
Son Jeremiah Maynor, 5 shillings.
Daughter Jemimah Maynor feather bed and 25 pounds money.
Daughter Rody Maynor, calf, feather bed when she reaches
the age of 16.
Son Stephen Maynor all the land on Smith River opposite
Bowen Creek to Edward Philpott's line and the rest of the
household items.
Lend to my loving wife Ann Maynor, the land that I now
live on and furniture.
Executors: Wife Ann Maynor, Isaiah Maynor and Stephen
Maynor to be joint executors.
Witness: John Philpott, Samuel Philpott and Josiah Turner.
Returned: July Ct 1798

Pg 31   Date: 26 July 1798
Item: Bond of Ann Maynor, Stephen Maynor, John Philpott,
Joseph Cummings. Ann Maynor and Stephen Maynor executors
of the estate of Richard Tucker Maynor.
Returned: July Ct 1798

Pg 32   Date: none
Item: Accounts current of the estate of Samuel King.
Includes: Furniture, gun and household items.
No Total.
Exhibited by Isam Craddock.
Returned: Sept Ct 1797

Pg 32   Date Jan 1797
Item Estate of Sameul King to Isam Craddock.
Attending S. King and his wife for 25 days and nights,
5 times going to the Mill, man and horse.
Making 2 coffins and finding planks.
1 Winding Sheet
Digging two graves
Taking an account of his goods.
Total 5.5.0.

Pg 33   Date: 25 Sept 1800
Item: Bond of Barnard M. Price and Moses Walden.
Price the administrator of the estate of_____.
Returned: Sept Ct 1800

Pg 34   Date: 29 July 1801
Item: Bond of Ruth Penn, George Penn, William Hanah, Gabriel Penn, Samuel Staples, Joseph Stovall, Brett Stovall, Robert Rowan, William Carter, Josiah Farris, John Frans and Hamon Critz.
Ruth Penn, George Penn and Gabriel Penn administrators of the estate of Abraham Penn deceased.
Witness: James Turner, James Carland and John Finney.
Returned: July Ct 1801.

Pg 35   Date: none
Item: Bond of Rachel Beller, Eli Beller and Edward Tatum. Rachel Beller and Eli Beller administrators of the estate of Elijah Beller.
Witness: Nathaniel H. Claibone
Returned: Sept Ct 1801

Pg 36   Date: 27 Oxr 1801
Item: Inventory of the estate of Elijah Beller, deceased.
Includes: Furniture, livestock, plantation equipment, Bible, dictionary, other books, half dozen Delf Plates.
No total included.
Appraisers: Bartlett Smith, Moses Freeman, Richard Atkinson.
Returned: Oct Ct 1801.

Pg 37   Date: 15 May 1801
Item: Inventory of the estate of Benjamin Martin.
Appraisers: James Ingrum, Isam Craddock and returned by William Via.
Items nor amountlisted.
Returned: Sept Ct 1801.

Pg 37   Date: 24 Aug 1801
Item: Will of Ann Easley
Legatees: My son Warham Easley, my feather bed. Daughter Judith Gains, a hatchet and kitchen furniture. The balance of the estate to remain unmolested until 1 November next, when it is to be sold to the highest bidder and the money derived to be divided between my son John Easley and my daughter Sucky Frances.
Executors: Sons Warham and Joseph Easley.
Witness: John Nunns and William Williams.
Returned: Oct Ct 1801.

Pg 38　　　　　　　　　　　Date: Oct 1801
Item: Bond of Warham Easley, Joseph Easley and James S. Gaines, Warham Easley and Joseph Easley the administrators of the estate of Ann Easley.
Returned: Oct Ct 1801.

Pg 39　　　　　　　　　　　Date: 7 Nov 1801
Item: Inventory of the estate of Ann Easley, deceased.
Includes: 1 negro woman, horses, saddle, grindstone and $220. in cash. A total of $449.40.
Appraisers: Warham Easley and Joseph Easley.
Returned: Nov Ct 1801.

Pg 40　　　　　　　　　　　Date: 25 Mar 1782????
Item: Bond of George Penn, Gabriel Penn and Joseph Stovall. George Penn administrator of the estate of Isaac Hollandsworth deceased.
Returned: March Ct 1802.

Pg 41　　　　　　　　　　　Date: 17 Jan 1802
Item: Will of Elizabeth Owens
Legatees: My son Leonard Owen for his particular care and attention in my old age, all of my estate consisting of my husbands fortune and stock. The other children are to have no part or share.
Witness: Thomas A......, Jean Dickerson, James Dickerson, Leonard Owen executor.
Rt: April Ct 1802.

Pg 42　　　　　　　　　　　Date: 10 Nov 1802
Item: Will of John Hancock, being in good health and perfect sense.
Legatees: Son Lewis to have land in Fluvanna County where I did live. Lend to my wife (not named) the whole estate during her life and widowhood and after her decease to: Son William, part of the land whereon I now live, from the end of the Mill Dam on the ridge to the north line. Son Major, the remaining part from there down. My son Benjamin, my wearing clothes.
After the decease of my wife, the rest of the estate to be divided between my five daughters and my son William. to wit; Nancy Corn, Rodue Lane, Elizabeth Mayo, Judith Mayo and Susannah Hancock and a proportionable part to my daughter Mary Morrison's two eldest children, Allen and Jincy Morrison.
Witness: John Scott and Mary Thompson
Executor: Son, William Hancock
Returned: Dec Ct 1802.

Pg 43   Date: 18 Jan 1802
Item: Will of John Breden, Sr., being weak of body....
Legatees: son John Breden 1 shilling sterling
          daughter Mary Breden the same
          son Isaac Breden the same
          son Joseph Breden the same
          daughter Margret Breden feather bed and furniture. Daughter Agnes Breden feather bed and furniture. Daughter Darcus Breden feather bed and furniture. Son James Breden to have one years schooling and a horse, saddle, bridle, but the horse is not to go out of the family. Dear and beloved wife Jean Breden to have one roan mare, saddle, feather bed, furniture, cattle and the rest of the estate to dispose of as she thinks fit.
Executors: Beloved sons Isaac and Andrew Breden and wife Jean Breden.
Witness: James Reynolds, Adam Turner and Bennet Houchins.
Returned: Feb Ct 1802.

Pg 44   Date: 2 Oct 1801
Item: Inventory of the estate of Abraham Penn, deceased.
Includes: 20 negros, horses, 27 chairs, 9 beds, 2 black walnut folding tables and two square ones, 1 black walnut cupboard, 1 old cherry desk, 1 rifle gun, 1 old smooth bore gun, glassware, books, looking glass, 1 black walnut bedstead and furniture and curtain, chests, a tea table, 1 sword blade, pair of money scales and weights, looms,etc.
Total: 1,829.15.10½.
Appraisers: James Taylor, Peter Frans, John Finney.

Pg 45   Date: 1 April 1802
Item: Inventory of the estate of Isaac Hollandsworth.
Includes: household furniture, horse, livestock, farm equipment and one dutch plow.
Total: 29.15.0.
Appraisers: John Gossett, David Baker, Joseph Cummings.

Pg 46   Date: none
Item: Inventory of the estate of John Hancock, deceased.
Includes: cattle, horses, plantation equipment, household furniture, sheep, books. Also, cotton due from George Lain. 8-3/4 gal. brandy due from W.J.Mayo, also same amount due next October.
Total: $382.17
Appraisers: David Harbour, Moses Harbour, Dandridge Slaughter.

Pg 46b   Date: 15 Jan 1803
Item: Account of the estate of John Hancock by William
Hancock, executor.
1 bond on Elephaz Shelton
2 bonds on Dandridge Slaughter, one due next Christmas
and one due October next.
One note on Joseph Saunders also an account due
An account against James Bolling
An account against William Salsberry
An account against William Handy
Sales to: James Whalen, James Moles, James Bolling,
William J. Mayo and Samuel Lain.

pg 47   Date: 30 Dec 1802
Item: Bond of William Hancock, John Hall and Matthew
Morrow. William Hancock the executor of the estate of
John Hancock.
Returned: Dec Ct 1802.

Pg 48   Date: 31 Mar 1803
Item: Bond of William Collings and William Carter.
William Collings the administrator of the estate of
Thomas Collings, deceased.
Returned: March Ct 1802.

Pg 49   Date: 5 April 1803
Item: Will of John Ellyson, being in a low state of
health....
Legatees: daughter, Sally Ellyson to have two hundred
pounds current money of Virginia.. The executor to pay
one half the expense of a new meeting house for the Dan
River Meeting when they build. As to my dear and beloved
wife (not named) provisions were made by a covenant before
our marriage, which was to be a provision for her and
also a bar against her right of dower. This is in the
hands of Joel Saunders and Barnabas Coffin who promised to
have it recorded in Guilford Court.
The remainder of my estate is intended for my son Thomas
Ellyson who is in a low state of health of a comsumptive
complaint. My executor is to provide and furnish my son
with every necessary and convenience of life that may
make his life more easy without regard to expense. Should
he recover so as to marry and have issue then to him and
his heirs. There are bonds on Thomas and Amos Ladd and
one on Nathan Dell for ten years. My executor is to
collect the interest for the estate (Executor to receive
$50.00 annually for his care of the bonds).

Should my son die, the money is to be used for the relief
of the poor and distressed of every sect and denomination.
I am too far reduced in a state of weakness to decide how
to place the money to best advantage, therefore it is
left to the Quarterly Meeting of which I am a member, to
act, knowing it is my desire that it be applyed to
charitable uses.
Executor: William Jessop
Witness: Jesse Williams, Robert Hudspeth and William Carter
Returned: June Ct 1803
Note: William Jessop refused to take the executorship, son
Thomas Ellyson appeared and was granted same.

Pg 50   Date: 30 June 1803
Item: Bond of Thomas Ellyson, Jonathan Hanby, Nathaniel
Smith, John Hughes and John Armstrong. Thomas Ellyson
to make an account of the estate of John Ellyson.
Returned: June Ct 1803.

Pg 51   Date: July 1803
Item: Sale of the estate of Alexander Trent, deceased.
Gun and horse, total 12.3.0.

Pg 51   Date: July Ct 1803
Item: Sale of the estate of Garrett Stoe, furniture
5.5.01.

Pg 52   Date: 20 Jane 1793
Item: Inquisition
Inquistion taken at the home of Francis Barrott before
Edward Tatum a Commissioner, on the when, where, how and
after what manner the said Francis Barrott came to his
death. Peter Bowman inflicted wounds that led to the
death of the said Francis Barrott.
Jurors: George Carter, Foreman
William Carter, Robert Hall, Sharp Benton, Jacob Lawson,
John Sharp, William Barton, Jacob Adams, Sr., Woody
Burge, Rodham Littrell, Golden Davidson and Eliphaz
Shelton.

Pg 53   Date: 9 Nov 1793
Inquistion taken at the plantation of Shadrack Going
before Edward Tatum a Commissioner. The body of
Nathan Going then and there lying dead. One Robert
Hall on Saturday 21 September last on the plantation

of Jacob Lawson mortally wounded the said Going on the head with a weeding hoe and broken the skull of Going, through the rage and passion of Robert Hall.
Jurors: Jonathany Hanby, Foreman
Obadiah Hudson, Isaac Pennington, Aaron Rea, Harberd Smith, Warham Easley, William Easley, Thomas Collings, William Collings, Anthony Collings, John Wilson and Richard Davidson.

Pg 54   Date: 24 June 1801
Item: Will of Abraham Frazer
Legatees: The perishable part of the estate to my son Abraham Frazer except to granddaughter Ellenor Turner one pided heffer calf after she comes of age. My son Abraham is to to sell no part of his property without the consent of my son Thomas Frazer. My daughter Polly to receive five shillings. The land is to be sold and the money equally divided between my two sons Abraham and Thomas. My wife shall keep in her possession this property during her lifetime and widowhood.
Witness: Thomas Frasure, John Webb and Joseph Smith.
Returned: Dec Ct 1802.

Pg 55   Date: 29 Mar 1798
Item: Bond of James S. Gaines, William Carter and Joshua Rentfro. James S. Gaines executor of the estate of Peter Sammons.
Returned: March Ct 1798

Pg 56   Date: 28 July 1803
Item: Guardian Bond of Thomas Parr and Gabriel Penn. Thomas Parr to see after the estate of Henry Parr, deceased for the heirs until of lawful age, these being: John Parr, Jr., Nancy Parr and Mazey Parr, children of Henry Parr, deceased.

Pgs 57 & 57a   Date: 26 July 1803
Item: Inventory of the estate of John Ellyson.
Contains: livestock, household items, silver watch, tea-pot and cups, Delf Plates, books, Johnson's dictionary, Stark's Justice, one Testament and one Rule of Life. Total: $461.62
Appraisers: Robert Hudspeth, Eli Beller and James Gaines.
Returned: July Ct 1803.

Pg 58   Date: 25 Aug 1803
Item: Bond of William Baker and James Baker.
William Baker the executor of the estate of David Baker, deceased, to make an inventory.
Returned: Aug Ct 1803

Pg 59   Date: 27 July 1803
Items: Inventory of the estate of Thomas Collings.
Contains: Livestock, furniture, household items, one large Bible, one Hym and one History.
Total: $210.37
Appraisers: Nathaniel Smith, Andrew Joyce, William Smith, William Burge.
Returned: Aug Ct 1803.

Pg 60   Date: 29 Sept 1803
Item: Bond of Jane Breden, John Breden, Alexander Lacky and Jesse Corn. Jane Breden the executor of the estate of John Breden, deceased.
Returned: Sept Ct 1803.

Pg 61   Date: 8 Dec 1798
Item: Will of Joseph Hale
Legatees: To my loving wife Rachel Hale the use of my whole land and plantation during her lifetime and the household furniture and all my stock.
The following children to receive five shillings: Thomas Hale, Joseph Hale, Mary Huff, Richard Hale, John Hale, Peter Hale, Rachel Parker, Sally Tittle. Elizabeth Hale and Nancy Hale. Daughter Keziah Hale to receive five pounds. My son Benjamin Hale is to receive all my land after my wife's death.
Witness: Benjamin Hale and Nancy Hale
Returned: Sept Ct 1803

Pg 62   Date: 27 Oct 1803
Item: Bond of Nancy Carter, John James and Jedediah Carter. Nancy Carter is the administrator of the estate of _____. (Pg 66 indicates Harris Carter is the deceased).
Returned: Oct Ct 1803

Pg 63   Date: 2 Nov 1803
Item: Inventory of the estate of John Breden.
Includes: Livestock, household items, furniture and
sundries of old books. ____money of North Carolina,
an "agr." of John Flanigan in 1775, and "adgr" on
Charles Evens in 1780. Notes on James Breden, John
Breden, Jr., John Norton an account of John Turner.
Total: $813.92
Appraisers: Adam Turner, James Turner, Jesse Corn.
Returned: Nov Ct 1803

Pg 64   Date: 24 Nov 1803
Item: Statement of Vouchers of the estate of
Elijah Beller, deceased.
Feb 1803 - Joseph Bannister
Feb 1801 - Peter Beller
    1803 - Caleb Summers and Jacob McCraw
    1801 - Elijah Rowark and Benjamin Carr
    1802 - Jeremiah Gibson and James Steward
    1800 - Nancy Beller
    1798 - Edward Tatum
    1800 - John Martin and William Steel
    1800 - Note of Hand
    1793 - Balance of Note
Proven account of Rhode Moore.
Returned: Nov Ct by Eli Beller, administrator.

Pg 65   Date: 21 Sept 1803
Item: Will of John Edens being very sick and weak.......
Legatees: My land is to be equally divided between my
three sons. Eldest son, his part on the creek above the
plantation. Second son, his part south, called "gum
holler." Third son possessth the part whereon the
house and plantation is contained to have at the death
of his mother. Frances, Mary and Nancy one shilling
apeace. Unto son David, one horse to be equal with the
one son John had. To duaghter Agness, one cow and
calf. To Ledy one cow and coalf, to Sary one cow and
calf, to Tabytha one cow and calf. Wife,   Elexander
and Elizabeth to have the rest of the cattle, hogs,
horses and household items. The same is not to be
interrupted until my wife's decease.
Executor: wife, Nancy Edens
Witness: Stephen Hubbard, Benjamin Hubbard and John
Conner.
Returned: Dec Ct 1803

Pg 66   Date: 29 Oct 1803
Item: Inventory of the estate of Harris Carter deceased.
Includes Livestock and furniture
No total
Appraisers: Joseph Cummings, Adren Anglin and Nathaniel Ross.

Pg 67   Date: 21 Nov 1803
Item: Sales of the estate of Harris Carter, deceased.
Livestock, furniture and a pair of spectacles.
Total: 129.3.6.
Nancy Carter, Administratrix
Rt: Dec Ct 1803

Pg 68   Date: 23 Feb 1804
Item: Bond of Benjamin James Harris, George Penn, William Carter, James S. Gaines and Brett Stovall. Benjamin J. Harris administrator of the estate of John Ellyson.
Returned: Feb Ct 1804

Pg 69 - Blank

Pg 70   Date: 3 Dec 1803
Item: Memorandum of sale of the property of David Baker, deceased at the house of William Baker.
Sold to William Baker, a still, horse and a chair.
To German Baker a saddle.
Total: 25.14.6
William Witt, Actionr.
Returned: Feb Ct 1804

Pg 71   Date: 3 Feb 1804
Item: Bond of Benjamin James Harris, Samuel Staples, James McCampbell. Benjamin J. Harris the administrator of the estate of Thomas Ellyson.
Returned: Feb Ct 1804.

Pg 72   Date: 27 July 1804
Item: Bond of Judith Quarles, James Quarles and Abraham Quarles. Judith Quarles the administratorix of the estate of _____.
Returned: July Ct 1804

Pg 73   Date: 1 Oct 1803
Item: Will of Francis Turner, being in perfect sense but weak in body......
I give and lend unto my well beloved wife during her natural lifetime, the land and plantation I now live on lying below a line beginning at a small branch south of Smith River at Thomas Flower's corner to Burnetts Santee place, also all the slaves and their increase excepting Bolin.
To my daughter Esther Pilson to have the twenty two pounds her husband William Pilson owes me for a mare, also to have a hundred pounds bond due me from Rowan and Scott. If Bolin is living at my death, he is to be sold and the price of him equally divided between the children of the said daughter.
Son Adam Turner, one negro, my still and all vessells and at his Mothers death one negro girl. I lend him a negro boy until his son Francis arrives at the age of 21, then to him. If Francis should die, then sell him and divide the money amongst his brother and sisters. To son James Turner, the original survey he now lives on (175 acres) also 2 tracts in Montgomery County containing 399 acres, and at his Mothers death three slaves.
To my son John Turner, the part of the tract I now live on lying above the line described earlier, two negros at his Mothers death, and I lend him one negro until his son Francis reaches age 21.
To my sons Adam, James and John Turner and my son-in-law Robert Rowan all that part of land lying on the Blue Ridge except 250 acres belonging to Robert Rowan. This contains 1223 acres and to be equally divided.
To my daughter Betsy Rowan at her mothers death all the part of the plantation that was to my wife.
To my dear wife during her natural lifetime all the house furniture, farming tools with all stock that be on hand after Esther Pilson is paid.
I leave ten pounds cash to support supplies or members of the Old Presbyterian Denomination at $4.00 per year.
Executors: sons Adam, James and John Turner.
Witness: William J. Mayo, Bennet Houchins, William Hancock, Richard Thomas and Alexander Lacky.
Returned: Oct Ct 1804.

Pg 74   Date: 27 Dec 1804
Item: Bond of Adam Turner, James Turner, John Turner, Robert Scott and William Banks. Adam, James and John Turner being the executors of the estate of Francis Turner.
Returned: Dec Ct 1804.

Pg 75   Date: 28 Feb 1805
Item: Bond of Claiborn Shelton and Eliphaz Shelton.
Claiborn Shelton the executor of the estate of
Coss Abraham, deceased.
Returned: Feb Ct 1805.

Pg 76   Date: 3 March 1798
Item: Inventory of the estate of Archelaus Hughes.
Contains: 18 negros, horses, cattle, hogs, plantation
tools, one desk and bookcase, looking glass, tea
table, silver watch, 45 books of different kinds,
money scales, one seal-skin trunk, 9 feather beds and
furniture, 18 blue rim plates, 3 french enamelled
mugs, wine glasses and other household items.
Total: 1616.2.5½.
Appraisers: Josephn Stovall, Richard Mills and Hamon
Critz.
Returned: May Ct 1805

Pg 77   Date: 1 April 1805
Item: Inventory of the estate of Coss Abram.
Includes livestock, farming equipment and one
tommahack. Total 45.17.5
Appraisers: Samuel Staples, William Witt and
George Fulcher.
Returned: May Ct 1805

Pg 78   Date: 29 Aug 1805
Item: Bond of Nancy Akers, James Via, Charles Foster,
Greensville Penn, Jesse Corn Sr., William Thompson.
Nancy Akers the administrat rix of Stephen Akers,
deceased.
Returned: Aug Ct 1805.

Pg 79   Date: Oct Ct 1805
Item: Account of John Lackey, deceased, by Peter
Saunders the Administrator.
By cash to Humphrey Smith
same to John Poteet
to Edward Lewis
to Gardner P. Morgan and Con. Morgan.
Expenses to Richmond paid to George Lackey and John
Koger. 1792 tobacco to Manchester.

Pg 80, 81   Date: 4 June 1805
Item: Will of Shadrack Going, being sick and weak.....
Legatees: To my beloved wife Hannah one feather bed,
furniture, kitchen furniture, "youse" of one sorrell
mare and possession of my house and her support out
of my plantation during her natural lifetime and at
her death her bed, furniture, etc to be "ekwill"
divided between Jerushe and Keziah Going.
The plantation whereon I now live on both sides of
Little Dan River to my beloved son Obediah, also my
hackle and one sorrell stud, mare and colt. His
mother is to have the use of the mare when she wishes.
Also to him bed, furniture, farm working tools, four
head of cattle, all hogs, in order to support himself
and his mother.
To my beloved daughter Keziah Going, one rone horse,
saddle, birdle, one cow bed and furniture.
To Rebecca Going, daughter of Fanny Going, wife of
Edmond Bowlin, one cow.
To following beloved sons five shillings each, to wit:
John Going, David Smith Going, Claborne Going, Soloman
Going, Shadrack Going and Caleb Going. To daughter
Fanny Bowlin, wife of Edmund Bowlin, five shillings.
To daughter Hannah Beazley, wife of Thomas Beazley
five shillings.
My upper plantation on the south side of Little Dan
River I have already given to Shadrack Beazley, son of
Thomas Beazley by deed.
Executors: William Carter and William Burge.
Witness: David P____, William Coomer, H____Adams.
Returned: Dec Ct 1805

Pg 82   Date: 4 June 1805
Item: Will of Bethany (Bethary) Haynes.
Mary Jones of Surry County, North Carolina came forth
and makes oath of the last will and testament of
Bethany Haynes.
To son Joshua all that part of land that lies on the
north side of the old spring branch to the big branch
called Sooks Branch.
The balance of the land divided between my four sons,
Bethany Haynes, William Haynes, Lyles (?) Haynes and
Joshua Haynes. With the following rescue??, that his
wife Morning Haynes have the household furniture and
stock and a third part of the produce raised on the
plantation.
Returned: Jan Ct 1806.

Pg 88   Date: 27 Mar 1805
Item: Bond of William Carter and John Hughes.
William Carter executor of the estate of Shadrack Going, deceased.
Returned: March Ct 1806.

Pg 84   Date: May Ct 1806
Item: Inventory of Shadrack Going, deceased.
Contains five books, household items and livestock.
Total: $289.13.
Appraisers: Nathaniel Smith, James L. Gaines and Samuel Hanby, Jr.

Pg 85   Date: 23 Sept 1805
Item: Inventory of the estate of Stephen Akers, deceased.
Contains livestock, household items - no total.
Appraisers: John Turner, David Harbour, William Burnett.
Returned: May Ct 1806

Pg 86   Date: 27 Mar 1806
Item: Guardian Bond of Gab. Penn and Robert Rowan.
Gabriel Penn as guardian for Edmund Penn and Phillip Penn, children and heirs of Abraham Penn, deceased.
Returned: March Ct 1806.

Pg 87   Date: 31 July 1806
Item: Bond of George Penn and Samuel Staples.
George Penn the administrator of the estate of Phillip Penn, deceased.
Returned: July Ct 1806.

Pg 88   Date: 7 Feb 1806
Item: Will of John Parr, Jr.
Legatees:
To beloved daughter Ann, a feather bed and furniture, a cow and calf.
To beloved son, William a cow and calf
To beloved son Mark a feather bed furniture and a cow and calf.
To beloved son Smith a feather bed furniture and a cow and calf.
To beloved daughter Sary(Sarah) the same
To beloved daughter Mary, the same
To beloved daughter Cindy M. the same
To beloved son Isham the same and one horse.

=20=

To my beloved son John E. Parr, feather bed and furniture,
a cow and calf and one horse.
To my beloved son Thomas Parr, feather bed and furniture,
cow and calf.
To my beloved wife Mary the use of my property, but not to
sell, rent or give any property away. At her death all
personal estate must be sold at public sale and the money
divided by the beloved children as follows:
Landall Tatum, Susannah Webb, Jean Colier, William Parr,
Ann Parr, Mark Parr, Sarah Parr, Isham Parr, Mary Parr,
Cindy M. Parr, John E. Parr and Thomas Parr.
Executors: William Smith, Jr., and John Smith.
Witness: James Epperson Jr, James Epperson, Sr., and
Thomas Haines.
Returned: Oct Ct 1806.

Pg 90, 91   Date: 2 Oct 1806
Item: Will of Isaac Adams being weak in body but in perfect
sense.....
Legatees:
To wife Hannah my bay mair Wilkes, a feather bed and
furniture and she is to continue onthe plantation.
My sons: Joseph Adams, Thomas Adams and Elisha Adams
all my lands and slaves.
To my daughter Leathey Adams, feather bed and furniture
and slaves.
To my daughter Polly Adams a negro.
To my son William Adams one bay mare 2 years old and
nothing more.
The remainder of the estate to remain on the plantation
for the support of the children who stay.
Executor: brother William Adams, Sr., and Brett Stovall.
Witness: w. Banks, Nancy Adams, Susannah Adams and
Nancy Barton.
Add: Son William Adams is to leave the plantation for
his disobediance to me.
Returned: Nov Ct 1806.

Pg 92, 93   Date: 1 April 1806
Item: Will of William Robertson, weak in body......
Legatees:
To Joel Chitwood a tract of land that fell to me by my
wife Nancy, being on the Pigg River in Franklin County.
To my brother George Robertson land that fell to me
out of the estate of my father in Franklin County on
Blackwater (River).
To my wife Nancy land in Franklin County on Little Outer
(Otter) Creek being on which I formerly lived. Also
land I now live on (266 acres) in Patrick County on

both sides of Smith River.
To my eldest daughters Rebeccah and Nancy, land on the north side of Smith River.
To my sons William Robertson and Benjamin Skinner Robertson land on the south side of Smith River.
To my three youngest daughters Ginea, Sally and Elizabeth all the stock and household furniture.
Executor: Benjamin Hancock and my wife Nancy Robertson.
Witness: John Sneed, Sally Fuson and Thomas Fuson.
Returned: Nov Ct 1806

Pg 95   Date: 19 April 1807
Will of Meredith Smith
Legatees: wife Lucy all my estate and at her death to be divided between all my children except Mary and Rebeccah who are to get $10.00 each less, because of the property they have already received.
Executors: friends Nehemiah Daniel and Robert Commons.
Witness: John Smith and John Eaton.

Pg 95   Date: 1805
Will of James Taylor, weak in body but in perfect sense...
Legatees: Sole and whole estate to dear and well beloved wife during her natural lifetime. Negro Hannah is to be emancipated, liberated and set free at my wife's death.
To my son James, after his mothers death, land and plantation whereon I now live.
To my son David, first choice of my three negros.
To my daughter Elenor Adams, third choice
To my son James Taylor, second choice
My personal estate to be sold after the death of my wife and equally divided amongst my daughters: Grizzle Collier, Virlinda Cummings her part is to remain in possession of the executor for her support as she needs it. Mary Lockhart (also spelled Lockart) and Milly Reynolds.
Executors: son David Taylor and son-in-law John Adams.
Witness: Samuel Staples, Henry Koger, John Koger Jr.

Pgs 96,97   Date: 27 Oct 1807
Will of Jacob Adams, being in a low state of health...
Legatees: to my beloved wife Mary the plantation where I now live, all my working tools and household and kitchen furniture, five negros, a bay mare, 4 cows and calfs, all sheep and hogs and all debts Thomas Reeves owes me, to her without controls during her widowhood.
To my son Jacob Adams a negro.
To my son Peter Adams a negro.
To my daughter Mary Cooper a negro.

To my daughter Lydda Tittle a negro. To my daughter ElizabethKeaton a negro, but not at all at the disposal of her husband Zackariah Keaton.
To my daughter Rebeccah Hollandsworth a negro, but not be at the disposal of her husband James Hollandsworth.
To my daughter Sarah Keaton a negro, but not to be at the disposal of her husband Cornelius Keaton.
To my son William Adams a negro.
To my son Isaac Adams a negro, a horse, feather bed and furniture.
Frances Cockrel is to have a horse valued at twenty five pounds.
Executors: friends Charles Foster and Capt. John Turner.
Witness: James Cox, Thomas Hill, Daniel Macantire.
Returned: Dec Ct 1807.

Pg 98 continuation of the estate of James Taylor found on pg 95.

Pgs 99,100   Date: 6 Oct 1808
Item: Will of Beveridge Hughes, being sick and weak....
Legatees:
Wife Nancy Hughes to have lifetime possession of the estate for support and to school children.
Son Blackmore Hughes land beginning at the first branch above the mansion house...to the path that used to go to Martin Lawrence's old place, when he arrives of age to take possession.
To son Beveridge Hughes land adjoining the above. Both sons to share the still at the death of their mother. Other good and chattels to be divided among children, to wit: daughter Martha Burnet, Agnes Hughes, Nancy Hughes, Sarah Hughes, Polly Hughes.
Witness: James Morrison, William Parmer, Sr., Elizabeth Thompson.
Returned: Oct Ct 1808.

Pg 101   Date 11 Sept 1803
Item: Will of William Barton
Legatees: wife Seppy Barton to have an equal part with the ten children or thirds. The estate to be sold and equally divided. If wife Seppy takes a third, then at her death, her part to be equally divided.
Children: William Barton, Susannah Davis, Sarah Adams, Betsy Strudhouse, Molly Keaty??, Jane Haile, Patsy Barton, Lydda Barton, Thomas Barton, Sharp Barton and daughter Nancy to have five pounds as her full share.
Executors: Thomas Barton and Sharp Barton.
Witness: Samuel Staples, John Hughes, Alexander Finney.

Pg 102
Codacil to the Will of William Barton dated 30 Nov 1807.
I have conveyed to George Penn for the benefit of Benjamin
Haile a tract of land sufficient for the proportion be-
queathed to my daughter Jane Haile, so I revoke the part
given to her in my will.
Witness: John Nunns, John Clark, William Clark.
Returned: Jan Ct 1808.

Pg 103   Date: 20 Jan 1808
Item: Will of John Parr
Legatees: To my wife Miriam Parr the land I live on
containing 188 acres with all personal estate, but she
is not to sell, give or rent the land. At her death all
personal estate to be sold and the money divided between
the children and grandchildren, to wit:
son Arthur Parr, son Noah Parr, daughter Mary Crump,
daughter Elizabeth Corn. My son John Parr, Jr., is
deceased and his part is to go to his living children.
To Miriam Fletcher, deceased, children of hers to have
her part.
My son Noah Parr to have land, but at his death, the
land is to go to his son Greensville Parr.
Executors: wife Miriam Parr, son Noah Parr, John Hughes.
Witness: John Smith, John Corn, Samuel Corn.
Returned: March Ct 1808.

Pg 104   Date: 23 Dec 1807
Item: Will of Thomas Hansby or Hensby
Legatees, dear and beloved wife Jemima Hensby to have
the estate, then at her death all the children to receive
the estate (not named).
Execuor: Jemima Hansby
Witness: James Spears, John Collings, Elijah Collings,
Thomas Isbell.
Returned: Feb Ct 1808.

Pg 105   Date: 28 June 1804
Item: Will of Benjamin Landrith, sick and weak in body..
Legatees, wife Hanna all my personal estate, then to the
children living with at the time of my decease and that
continue to live with my wife. Should any leave before
her death, they are to receive an equal part of the
estate. The land I live on is to go to my son McKindley
Landrith and my grandson Benjamin Ray after my wife's
death.
Witness: Gab. Penn, Samuel Staples, John Hansby, Sr.
Returned: March Ct 1808.

Pg 106   Date: 21 Aug 1807
Item: Will of James Goin
Legatees: Peggy Adams to receive twenty five dollars over and above what I have already given her. My daughter Prudence Goin to receive five shilling over and above what I have given her. Son Stephen to receive five shillings over and above what he has received. Son William is to receive $55.00 above what he has received. Daugther Betsy Goin is to receive $150.00 over and above what she has received. The above four are not to receive their part until the youngest children come of age. My widow is to take care of the estate, but should she remarry then the estate is to be taken out of her hands. The youngest children: Arthur, Isaac and Nancy Goin.
Executors: Jesse Williams, Joseph Jessup, Joseph Jackson, John A. Grigg.
Witness: Moses H. Grigg, Moses Grigg, Drury Bonduarant.
Returned: Jan Ct 1807.

Pg 107   Date: none
Item: Will of Robert Wright (Rite)
Legatees: Wife to have stock, furniture, her feather bed, at her death the negros, stock etc to be sold and monies divided amongst sons and daughters: John Wright, Josiah Wright, Reuben Wright, Mary Wright, Fanny Wright and Elizabeth is to have a negro at her mothers death.
Executor: wife and John Hall
Witness: George Pigg, Sarah Hall, John Hall
Returned: July Ct 1809

Pg 108   Date: 25 Oct 1809
Item: Will of Joshua Adams
Legatees: Wife Elizabeth to have all of the household furnishings during her lifetime, the rest of the estate to be sold and the money used to educate my son John Adams.
Executors: William Sneed and William Fuson
Witness: Thomas R. Hall, Major Hancock, James Fuson.
Returned: Nov Ct 1809

Pg 109   Date: 27 Feb 1811
Will of Silus (Silas) Ratliff, Sr.
Legatees: To my daughter Usley one cow and yearling, the balance of the estate to remain in the possession of my wife Elizabeth Ratliff and at her decease to be sold and divided amongst my children: John Ratliff, Silus Ratliff, Jr., Lydda Bryant, Fanny, Pheby, Hanah Harper, Usley and Mary Ratliff.
Witness: John Hall and Silas Ratliff, Jr.
Returned: April Ct 1811.

Pg 110   Date: 30 Sept 1808
Will of Frances Tucker
Legatees: My estate to be divided between my first six children, to wit: George Lee, Richard Lee, Elizabeth Crutcher, Susannah Harrison, Jane Tinsley and Nancy Tucker. My son Robert Tucker is to be paid out of the estate of his father.
Executor: My nephew George Penn and son-in-law Richard Harrison.
Witness: Brett Stovall, Thomas Penn, Hamon Critz.
Returned: Jan Ct 1812.

Pgs 111, 112   Date: 12 Feb 1813
Will of William Perkins, being sick and weak.....
The land I now live on sold and the money equally divided among my sons Christian, William, David and Thomas Perkins The land I own on the mountain is to be sold and divided amongst my daughters. Son Christian Perkins to have three negros. Son William one negro and fifteen pounds cash. Son Thomas two negros. Son David two negros. Daughter Sarah Reynolds two negros. Daughter Susanah two negros, two feather beds and furniture, one horse and side saddle. Daughter Elizabeth two negros, one feather bed and furniture and two mares. Daughter Nanney Boyd two negros. I lend to Mary Ann Moss one negro. It is my desire that the land Joseph Reynolds lives on to be sold and the money divided amongst all of his children. What I have not given away is to be sold and the money divided among my sons and daughters. The money coming to Sarah Reynolds to be put out to interest until her last child come of age then divided among them. The same applies to Nanny Boyd.
One daughter is mentioned as Suky.
Witness: Richard Stokes, Fanney Stokes, Sarah Hall.
Executor: John Hall and Samuel Houston
Returned: March Ct 1813.

Pgs 113, 114   Date 10 Aug 1808
Will of John Rusk, being old and infirm but of sound mind....
Legatees: beloved wife Nelly all the tract of land whereon I now live, all horses, cows and hogs, household and kitchen furniture together with all and every kind of property I possess during her natural lifetime.
To my wife's brother John Grey, one cow.
To Sally Campbell commonly called Sally Rusk, I do hereby recognize and acknowledge her as my child. All possessions at the death of my wife to go to Sally on the condition she remain with my wife. Should she mistreat my wife or leave her, she is not to receive the estate.

Executor: My wife Nelly Rusk.
Witness: P. R. Gilmer, Henry Koger, John Koger, Jr.
Returned: July Ct 1814.

Pg 114   Date: 27 March 1814
Will of McKindlay Landrith
Legatees: To Benjamin Landrith, Jr. all my part of the
land my father left me, all my clothes and one-half of
my living property.
To Hannah Owen, the other half of my living property.
To my brother Jonathan Landrith the sum that is due me,
about $24.00 or his account.
Executor: Elisha Bellar
Witness: John Smith, William McMillan, Munf. Smith
Returned: Feb Ct 1814.

Pg 115   Date: 3 July 1812
Will of John Brammer, Senr.
Legatees: Land is to be sold and the money divided
between my sons and daughters, to wit: daughter Sarah
Manning, son Birges(Burgess) Brammer, son Edward Brammer,
daughter Frankey, son John Brammer, Jr is to receive
$1.00. To my daughter Mary Manning my bed and furniture,
my rifle gun, my spoon moles, my clothes, shrouding dress
all now in the possession of John Brammer, Jr. Also she
is to receive the benefit of bonds deposited in the
possession of my son John Brammer, Jr, which bonds is now
detained from my benefit.
Executor: John Hall, Charles Thomas, Jr.
Witness: Agnes Chambers, Ann Herd, John Chambers, Hugh
Boyd, Francis Hughes.
Returned: Nov Ct 1813.

Pg 116   Date: 9 Nov 1812
Will of John Ingrum, Senr. being weak of body......
Legatees: To my dearly beloved wife Elizabeth, the
whole of my lands that I now live on, that is to say
my upper and lower plantation, household and kitchen
furniture, two negros and children, whole of my stock,
grain, corn. After her decease this is to be equally divided amongst my three daughters: Sarah Adams, Franky Mize
and Ruth Mize. The rest of the goods sold, but the negros
to remain in the family.
Executors: sons John and James Ingrum and wife Elizabeth.
Witness: William Walden and Margarett Walden
Returned: July Ct 1814.

Pg 117   Date: 20 Aug 1818
Will of Adron Anglin
The executor is to sell part of the estate and supply
money for the support of the children.
Legatees:
To my son Philip Anglin ten shillings
To my son John Anglin ten shillings
To my daughter Matilda Sharp ten shillings
To my daughter Elizabeth Anglin ten shillings
The remainder of my estate to be in the possession of
my wife until Lydia comes of age, then the estate is
to be sold and divided between my wife Elizabeth, Sr.,
my daughter Lydia Anglin, my daughter Jane Anglin, my
son Naaman Anglin and my son Elisha Anglin.
Executor: Greenville Penn
Witness: David Harbour, Moses Harbour, Naaman Harbour.
Returned: Sept Ct 1818.

Pgs 118-120   Date: 26 March 1819
Will of Ignatious Simms, being weak and afflicted in
body but with perfect and sound mind....
Legatees: To my wife Jannet I lend seven negroes, the
home tract of 588 acres and benefit of the grist mill
on Bowen's Creek, household and cupboard furniture,
kitchen furniture, plantation tools and my wife is to
raise the dear infant children.
To my well beloved daughter Polly Hagood two negros and
four children.
To my beloved daughter Ann Nance two negros
To my beloved daughter Elizabeth Hagood two negros
To my beloved daughter Elender Nance two negros
To my beloved daughter Exoney Simms two negros, one
feather bed and furniture, one horse, one cow and
calf, these when she arrives at the age of 18 or marries.
To my beloved daughter Marget Simms land on Bowin's Creek
whereon my Grist Mill stands adjoining Gregory Hagoods
line and Smith River also two negros, feather bed and
furniture, one horse, saddle bridle, one cow and calf,
these when she marries or becomes 18.
To my beloved daughter Jancee Foster 100 acres of land
adjoining Charles Foster to the corner between me and
Samuel Packwood, also two negros and three children.
To my son John Dabney Simms two negros, feather bed and
furniture, horse, saddle, bridle, cow and calf and a
rifle gun.
To my son William Robertson Simms the same as John when
he arrives at the age of 21 years.
To my son Ignatious Andrew Jackson Simms same as John
when he arrives at the age of 21 years.

To my son Marmaduke Manor Simms one tract of land, 152 acres near the head of Smith River in Patrick County beginning at Ward's corner line.
At my decease to John Dabney Simms, Ignatious A.D. Simms, and William R. Simms all of the land not otherwise disposed of.
Should my wife (Jannet) die before the children reach the age of 21, Edmund Nance and his wife to be the trustee and guardian for these children.
Executor: My wife Jannet, Gregory Hagood and Edmund Nance.
Witness: Eusebeus Stone, Micajah Stone, William Stone, Peter Smith.
Returned: Sept Ct 1819.

Pg 121   Date: 26 March 1817
Will of Jonathan Hanby, being sick and weak......
Legatees:
My beloved wife Sally to have the land and dwelling house whereon I now live, household furniture, kitchen furniture, stock of all kinds with five negros during her lifetime. At her death the land is to go to my son Gabriel Hanby. My still and smith tools are to remain on the plantation for the use of my wife and at ther death to be sold, this and the rest of the estate to be sold and the money divided amongst my children and the heirs of John Hanby who are: Polly, Sally, James, Peter and John.
My son Samuel one negro. To my son William Hanby, I give one negro, which he has sold. To my daughters: Susannah, Mary, Nancy, Jane and Sally I give four negros.
Executors: My sons Gabriel and William Hanby.
Witness: John Tatum, David Hanby, John Halbert.
Returned: May Ct 1817.

Pgs 122,123   Date: 11 Dec 1818
Will of William Jones, weak and low in body, but perfect sense.......
Legatees: To my beloved wife Ann, the land and plantation where I now live five negros, all stock, household and kitchen furniture. To my son Gabriel the land and plantation at the death of my wife and he is to have a tolerable good riding horse, saddle, bridle, cow and calf, pigs and five shoats, one feather bed and furniture when he arrives at the age of 21 years. To my daughter Nancy one negro, feather bed and furniture.
To my daughter Salley the same.
To my daughter Zilpha the same
To my daughter Winnefred Shelton Fifty dollars.

To my grandsons: William Shelton and John Shelton
$100.00 each.
Winnefred Shelton and Gabriel Jones to have their part,
the balance at the death of my wife is to be divided among
my other nine children to wit: Elizabeth Crowiher ??,
Polly Francis, Rachel Fulton, Augustine Jones, John Jones,
Lucy Philpott, Nancy Jones, Sally Jones, Zilpha Jones.
Executors: Augustine Jones, John Jones, John Francis.
Witness: Richard Harrison, William Thompson, William Carter
Returned: Feb Ct 1819

Pg 123   Date: 1818
Will of William Harris, weak in body......
Legatees: howle estate to my wife. My son Moses Harris
is to receive the land and plantation after his mothers
death.
Daughter Rebecah Harris is to have a feather bed and
furniture.
The rest to be divided between my four children, namely:
Rebeccah Harris, Moses Harris, Joel Harris and Elizabeth
Ayres.
Executors: David Taylor and son Moses Harris
Witness: Moses Cummings, Mary Spencer
Returned: April Ct 1818

Pg 124   Date: 12 May 1815
Will of Mary Frans being weak and low.....
My son Daniel Frans and my grandson Martin Miller are to
divide the entire estate between them.
Executors: Daniel Frans and Martin Miller.
Witness: George Penn, Josiah Ferris, Joseph Stovall.
Returned: Oct Ct 1817.

Pg 125   Date: 24 March 1816
Will of Noah Harbour, weak in body and feeble....
To my wife Mary Harbour during her lifetime to fully
enjoy the use of the plantation. Should there be no
ishew from her own body the one majority to my brothers.
If they are not then living, to the next of kin.
Executors: Thomas Harbour, Jeremiah Burnett, Jr., and
William Hancock.
Witness: Nathan Hall, Henry Thompson, James Keeth.
Returned: Aug Ct 1816

Pg 126   Date: 23 Oct 1815
Will of John Vanniel of the County of Montgomery,
State of Virginia.
All of the perishable part of the estate to be sold,
the money and the rest of the estate to be divided
amongst the children, to wit:
My son Tobias Vanniel, my son Samuel Vanniel, my son
John Vanniel, my son Jonas Vanniel, my daughter Mary
Vanniel late Thompson, my son Elias Vanniel, my son
Edmond Vanniel, my daughter Caty Vanniel late Saunders,
my son Isaac Vanniel and my son Adam Vanniel.
Witness: John Weddle, Augustine H. Smith, John Anglin.
Returned: April Ct 1817.

Pg 127   Date: 23 Feb 1815
Will of James Ingrum
Legatees: My son Alexander Ingrum two negros
My daughter Nancy Ross, two negros
My daughter Sarah Ingrum, two negros
My daughter Nancy Adams, two negros
My daughter Mary Ingrum two negros and land on the
south side of Smith River. At her marriage she is to
have a horse, saddle, feather bed and furniture, cow and
calf. To my son James Ingrum, two negros, land on the
north side of Smith River, bed and furniture, cow and
calf.
To my wife Martha Ingram all of the rest of my estate
during her widowhood and at her death: this to be
divided equally amony my children.
Executor: My wife and son Alexander Ingrum.
Witness: James Cox, Jacob Prillaman, Edward Lewis.
Returned: Oct Ct 1816

Pg 128   Date: 28 Oct 1816
Will of James Nowlin, being in a low state....
Legatees:
My wife Ursula to receive the whole of my estate and
after her death the estate to go to my grandson David
Nowlin, son of my son Samuel Nowlin.
Samuel Nowlin is to care for his mother and not let her
suffer from the want of anything.
Executor: Mathew Sandefer and James Boaz, Sr.
Witness: Jesse Atkinson, Joseph Atkinson, James Boaz, Jr.

Returned: Dec Ct 1816.

Pg 129   Date: 14 Jan 1814
Will of Sherad Harris, being weak.....
Legatees:
To my oldest son Claiborne Harris, my still with worm and head.
The balance of my estate is to remain with my wife to her death then be equally divided amongst my seven youngest children: Patsey, Robert, Polley, Salley, Bevin, Elijah and James. There is to be no division until the youngest comes of age.
Also: It is my desire that my four daughters, Dicy, Betsy, Charlot and Lyddy keep what they had at their marriage as their part and no more.
Executors: Samuel Howell and James Howell
Returned: May Ct 1814.

Pgs 129-130   Date: 19 Feb 1815
Will of Nathan Hall, being sick and weak....
Legatees:
John Hall is to have a portion of the land I now live on joining the land John bought from Benjamin Hubbard.
The balance of the estate, land and slaves to be sold and the money divided amongst my sons and daughters: Randal, Thomas, Jonathan, Molley, John, Sally, Nancy, Jeremiah and Frankey.
Executor: John Hall and Thomas R. Hall
Witness: Russell Hall, Delila Hall, Ann Hall
Returned: March Ct 1815

Pgs 131-132   Date: 29 Nov 1815
Will of William Smith, Sr.
Legatees:
To my son John the lower tract I now live on, desk, a negro in the possession of my wife to go to John at her death.
To my son Munford the upper part of the tract where I live after my wife's death and a small cubboard.
I lend to my wife two negroes, one best horse, one best mare cart, two work steers, blacksmith tools, four cows and calfs, four dry cattle, 20 head of hogs, 10 sheep, household and kitchen furniture..these during her lifetime then sold and divided among my children and grandchildren. A childs part to children and grandchildren: Henry Smith, Isaam Smith, Harbard Smith, Nathaniel Smith, Bartholomew Smith, John Smith, Munford Smith, Susanah Frans, William Parr, Nancy Parr, Smith Parr, Sinda M. Parr, John Edm. Parr, and one child's part to

be divided between Nancy E. Gilliam and Susanah Gilliam, one child's part divided between Gincy Lyon and Jacob Lyon.
Executors: Wife Hannah Smith and son John Smith.
Witness: William Jones, John Jones, Joseph Gray and William Frans.
ITEM: I lend my daughter Jean Gilliam a slave then to her children. To my daugher Mary Parr I lend two negros then to her children. To my daughter Ann Rogers I give one negro. To my daughter Susanah Frans one negro and one looking glass.
Returned: Feb Ct 1816.

Pg 133 Date: 4 Aug 1815
Will of John Sneed, Sr., being weak....
Legatees:
Wife Nancy Sneed to dispose of the estate as she sees fit.
To each child Fifty cents as follows:
To my eldest son William Sneed; to the heirs of my son Richard Sneed, deceased; to my son John Sneed; to my youngest son Samuel Sneed; to my daughter Patsey James, to my daughter Judith Packwood; to my daughter Nancy Carter; to my youngest daughter Janey Carter.
Executor: My eldest son William Sneed.
Witness: William Fuson, James Sneeed, Abraham Sneed.
Returned: Oct Ct 1815.

Pg 134 Date: 14 May 1820
Will of John Tuggle being weak in body...
Legatees:
My wife to have one sorrel horse I got from Capt. Richard Thomas. The estate divided between my wife and ten children, to wit:
Sally Jones, Mary Lee, Henry Tuggle, Elizabeth Bolling, Nancy Burnett, Frances Brammer, Lucy Brammer, James Tuggle, John Tuggle, Anne Sheeler and my wife Nancy Tuggle.
Executor: My friend Capt. Richard Thomas
Witness: M. Standefer, Robert Loyd, Samuel Harris
Returned: Sept Ct 1820.

Pg 135 Date: 8 Jan 1809
Will of John Camron
Legatees: Nieces and nephews, being the children of Joseph Cameron, deceased. To my two sisters Elizabeth and Frankey..all to receive one shilling each.
I give and bequeath to Ceasar Fendly a black man I raised and liberated about four years ago all my estate real or personal, all debts that are due me and everything else belonging to me.

Executors: Hamon Critze, George Penn, Sr., Richard Hopkins.
Witness: George Penn, Horatio Penn, James Penn and Joel Chitwood.
Returned: Nov Ct 1824.

Pg 136   Date: 13 Sept 1825
Will of Samuel C. Morris
Legatees:
To my son Benjamin Morris after the death of my beloved wife, all the tract on which I now live east of William Morris containing 200 acres.
At the death of my wife, to my daughter Rebecca Bradley the balance of my land, not before mentioned.
To my daughter Lucindy Handy, one negro.
To my son Samuel C. Morris $1.00
To my son William Morris $1.00
To my daughter Nancy Brown $1.00
To my son John Morris $1.00
All the balance of my estate not otherwise disposed of at the decease of my wife to go to my son Benjamin Morris. My daughter Polly Jarrett to receive $1.00. Wife's name Susanna Morris.
Executor: Son Benjamin Morris
Witness: William J. Mills, Thomas J. Morris, Taylor Abington.
Returned: March Ct 1826

Pg 137   Date: 25 Jan 1824
Will of John Rea being sick, weak in body but sound and perfect mind....
Legatees:
To my beloved wife Mildred Rea the whole of my estate, both real and personal during her natural lifetime. After the decease of my wife the whole of my personal estate to be equally divided between my three grandchildren: John, Lucinda and Andrew Leek and my nephew Hasley Rea. Should they die without issue the estate is to revert to my two brothers Joseph and David Rea. It is my desire that my nephew Horsley Rea continue to live with my wife and supperintend the estate during her lifetime. He is to receive $500.00 to be paid out of the value of my land. The land is to be equally divided between my grandchildren
Executor: Wife Mildred Rea and brother Joseph Rea
Witness: John Hughes and M. Sandefer
Returned: March Ct 1826.

Pg 138   Date: 19 Dec 1820
Will of William McAlexander, Sr. being sick and weak
but of sound mind....
Legatees: To my beloved wife Tamer my whole estate,
except for the sums I give my children as followeth:
My daughter Jane Morris $1.00 in money, daughter
Peggy Harris $1.00, daughter Esther Lackey $1.00, to
my son James McAlexander $1.00; to my son William
McAlexander $1.00; to my daughter Nancy Booth $1.00;
to my daughter Sarah Booth $1.00; to my daughter
Mary Boothe $1.00; to my daughter Elizabeth Carrol
$1.00; to my daughter Hannah Brammer $1.00; to my son
Alexander McAlexander 100 acres of land lying in the
face of the mountains and joins the land of John Tuggle,
deceased and John Tuggle, Jr. and $1.00 in money. To
my son John McAlexander one certain parcel of land by
the waters of Rock Castle Creek known by the name of
"Rich Hollow" to the ridge near William Harris' line.
To my sons John and and Samuel a piece of land known
as "Bob's Place" and bounded by the land of William
McAlexander on the north and by Bejah ? Boothe and
Gabriel Boling, William Ayres, John Massey and
Euritit?? Nance. To my daughter MillyMcAlexander a
negro girl. To my son David McAlexander my home tract
to near Bubby Blopans or Clopans(spelled both ways), to
the Elijah Dehart line, the land being on Rock Castle
Creek and also my still. To my son Samuel the rest of
my land theplace where the widow Auz?? formerly lived
adjoining the lands of Jesse Dehart, Elijah Dehart and
John Massey. To my other three daughters, Isabelah,
Tamer and Rachel, one negro each to be given by my
wife. To my beloved wife Tamer and also son Daniel part
of the land while she lives..should she remarry or at
her death. To my four daughters Milly, Isabel, Tamar
and Rachel one feather bed and furniture. The balance
of my estate to be equally divided amongst my children.
Executor: Wife Tamer McAlexander and Jesse Jones.
Witness: John Massey, William Ayres, Gabriel Boling.
Returned: March Ct 1822.

Pg 140   Date: 14 April 1821
Item: Will of James Bartlett, Sr
Legatees: Wife Temperance Bartlett during her natural
lifetime to have all my estate both real and personal.
At her decease the land to be annually rented for two
years, the money arising thereof divided equally between
my three daughters: Polly Breydon, Susanna Massey and
Nancy Massey. After two years the land to be sold and the
money equally divided amongst all of my children. The
whole of my personal estate (except negro Sam) I wish to

be sold. Pay out of such as my just debts, then pay each of my grandaughters Ann C. Bartlett and Nancy G. Bartlett, daughters of my son Thomas Bartlett, deceased the sum of $100.00. The balance remaining equally divided among all my children. My negro man Sam is not to be sold but live among my three children Susanna Massey, Nancy Massey and James Bartlett, Jr., beginning with the oldest then next and so on during his lifetime.
Executors: John Massey, Stephen Hubbard, Maes Bartlett.
Witness: M. Sandefer, William Canaday, Jeremiah Burnett and Fleming Hall.
Returned: Feb Ct 1823.

Pg 141   Date: 23 July 1824
Will of Samuel Packwood, sick and weak in body but of perfect mind.
Legatees: All of my estate both real and personal to be enjoyed by my well beloved wife Elizabeth Packwood during her natural lifetime, except such useless stock or other property as she may direct my executor to sell in order for distribution amongst the legatees. After the decease of my wife all lands except 63 acres lying on the south side of Smith River and adjoining land whereon Charles Smith now lives and being part of the land sold him by William and Elisha Packwood which rite and lawful title I want said Charles Smith to have. The balance of land is to be sold by the executors and divided as follows: Give the profit of said land equally to my children: William Packwood, Richard Packwood, Larkin Packwood, Samuel Packwood, Rachel Smith, Valentine Gearhart, Nancy Packwood for the benefit of Sally Bartlett's children, to Nancy Packwood for her own benefit, Edith McCutchen, Elizabeth Prillaman and Elisha Packwood. Elisha is to pay $100.00 out of his legacy to be divided among the rest named.
My daughter Nancy Packwood is to have a negro girl.
Executor: My daughter Nancy Packwood and neighbor Peter Smith.
Witness: Larkin Packwood, Grandason Lesuer, Richard Stone
Returned: Nov Ct 1825.

No page 142

Pg 143   Date: 17 Nov 1820
Will of Clement Rogers in a low state of health......
Legatees: to my beloved wife Ann Rogers the tract of land whereon I now live containing 209 acres with all worldly estate and property during her natural life or widowhood. As for the above land I give my wife power to sell or dispose of it. After her death all of the estate must be

sold at public auction and money divided between any children herein named: Elizabeth Boaz, David Rogers, Sarah S. Rogers, John S. Rogers. Elizabeth Boaz has had property that I gave her to the amount of $50.00 which is to be deducted out of the settlement with the others.
Executor: Wife Ann Rogers
Witness: John Smith and Abstam ? Shelton
Returned: Jan Ct 1823

Pg 144   Date: 13 Nov 1819
Will of John Adams being in a low state of health....
Legatees: I bequeath all my land, goods and chattels to my beloved wife Mary during her natural life or widowhood. My son Joshua Adams has had his at 200 (acres?) land, beast, saddle, cow and calf. To my daughter Elizabeth Corn a feather bed and furniture, beast, saddle and cow.
to Phebe Corn the same
To Sarah Spencer the same
to Mary Spencer the same
to Ann Nelson the same
It is my desire that my other three daughters have a bed, beast, saddle and cow, the same amount as the rest of my daughters. The land that was Joshua's, I bequeath to my son Paul C. Adams at two hundred dollars the piece and to have his bed, beast, saddle and cow. The tract I now live on is to be divided between my other three sons. Roland H. Adams is to begin at Marvel's fence, etc., he is to have his bed, beast, saddle and cow. The upper part is to James Adams to the mountain path, he is to have his bed, beast saddle and cow. The rest of the tract is for John J. Adams, the middle tract at 200 the piece, to have his bed, beast, saddle and cow and to have $100.00 more than the others as he is not able to labour for his liven in the field.
Executor: Wife Mary Adams and son Joshua Adams
Witness: Jesse Moore and Mary Moore
Returned: Jan Ct 1820

Pg 145   Date: 2 Jan 1806
Will of William Parmer, being well in body....
Legatees: Leave the entire estate to my children, to wit: John Parmer, William Parmer, Samuel Parmer, Malachi Parmer, David Parmer, Edward Parmer, Elizabeth, Sally, Susannah and Mary Parmer late Mary Hurt.
Executor: son-in-law Moses Hurt, son William Parmer
Witness: Dandridge Slaughter, Malachi Parmer, Archalous Bernard.
Returned: Dec Ct 1822 ((Also spelled Palmer in other records)

Pg 146   Date: 6 Oct 1819
Will of Milly Robertson
Legatees: To my beloved children Judith Turner, Lcuy Conner and David Robertson, Jr, each one-third of my estate.
Witness: Prier Pendleton, Benjamin Hubbard
Returned: Sept Ct 1820

Pg 147   Date: 24 June 1820
Will of John Brown, being advanced in years and afflicted in body....
Legatees: To my niece Betsey Brown my dark bay mare, one bed and furniture, one cow and calf. To my nephew Noah Brown one bed and furniture, one cow and calf.
To my beloved wife Mary all the balance of my estate to dispose of as she thinks proper.
Executor: Wife Mary Brown and Greensville Penn
Witness: John Redman, Caty Redman, L. P. Stovall
Returned: Oct Ct 1820

Pg 148   Date: 20 June 1816
Will of Richard Harrison weak and low in body....
Legatees: to my beloved wife Susannah Harrison during her natural life the land whereon I now live, six negroes, stock of every kind, household and kitchen furniture, plantation utensils, except what has been furnished my children that are married. To be delivered to my son Benjamin one negro whenever he wants it. To my granddaughter Susannah Frans, daughter of Hariette Frans, one negro which is to be accounted for as part of my daughter Hariett Frans' legacy. After my wife's death the estate is to be equally divided between my seven children: George Harrison, Nicholas Harrison, William Harrison, Francis Harrison, Richard Harrison, Benjamin Harrison and Hariette Frans. Deduct from George and Francis' part of estate $250.00 each for land which I gave them and add to Francis part $20.00, to Richard $50.00, this allowed to them to make their negros equal to the other children. Niece Polly Harrison is to receive twenty five pounds.
Executors: My sons Richard and Benjamin Harrison
Witness: George Penn, William Critz, Hamon Critz, Robert Boaz.
Returned: June Ct 1820

Pg 149   Date: 27 April 1822
Will of Augustine Thomas
Legatees: To my son Washington Thomas the land where he now lives, 216 acres.

=38=

To Benjamin Thomas' three sons, namely: James Waring Thomas, Robert Anderson Thomas and Augustine Thomas the.....tract of land that their deceased father had received with other property and $120.00 in cash. The hirschew(horseshoe?) tract of land I wish to be sold and the money put to interest until the youngest son Augustine comes of age. To Nancy Wade, daughter, a negro with stock and household furniture. To my daughter Rachel Thomas a negro, horse, saddle, feather bed and furniture and part of the cattle and sheep. To my daughter Mary Thomas two negros, mare colt, saddle, feather bed and furniture, part of the sheep and cattle. To my sons Edward and Augustine Bartholomew Thomas a negro and the place I now live on with all the rest of the out land belonging, all plantation tools, all smith tools, wagons, four horses, cattle, sheep, two feather beds and furniture and kitchen furniture. To my daughter Deborah Burrous two negros, stock and household furniture. My wife Deborah Thomas is to have her maintenance with every necessary for her comfortable living with a horse and saddle.
P.S. At my death all money that is left is to be equally divided between the four named children: Rachel, Mary, Edward and Barthalomew.
To my daughter Lucinda Cogar two negros, feather bed and furniture, a mare and saddle.
Witness: John Hughes, Samuel Hughes, John Rea.
Returned: May Ct 1822.

Pg 150   Date: 29 March 1826
Will of Jacob Hudson
Legatees: To wife Sally Hudson all real and personal property during her lifetime, at her death to be divided equally between the children. Son, William R. Hudson received property in 1814 of a negro $200.00, one horse, bed and furniture, cow and calf, sow and pigs, five head of sheep. Daniel Hudson received a negro, price $400.00, horse, cows, pigs, sheep all of which he received in 1819. Son David Hudson received a negro at $300.00 plus other things in 1819. Daughter Lucy R. Joyce received a negro at $300.00 plus other things plus $30.00 to make her equal with the others. To son John H. Hudson a negro at $250.00 plus other things received in 1826.
Executors: sons, Danniel and John H. Hudson
Witness: John Tatum and C. J. Terrell
Returned: May Ct 1826.

Pg 151   Date: 22 April 1826
Item: Will of William Gray being low in body but sound in mind.
To my beloved wife Mary all my lands in Patrick County and elsewhere, eleven negros, all the household furniture money and bonds that I have on hand. At her death, this is to be equally divided between all our children, except those I have given a negro or money. To Mary Dickerson's heirs, a negro; to Mary New a negro, to Nancy Taylor a negro, to Elizabeth Webb a negro. I wish the $233.00 which I lent my son James to be counted in when the estate is equally divided.
Executors: Reuben Taylor and Daniel Gray
Witness: Bird Lowe, George Gunter, Robert Lowe
Returned: May Ct 1826.

Pg 152   Date: 1808
Item: Sale from the Estate of William Deal, deceased. Sales to: William Penn, John Spencer, Soloman Keaton, William Keaton, Sally Deal, Lucy Deal, James Deal, John James, Thomas Penn, Hamon Critz, Townley Rigg.
Total: 7.10.12.
Returned: Feb Ct 1809.

Pg 153   Date: 18 Jan 1808
Item: Sales of the Estate of Francis Turner, deceased made by the consent of Elizabeth Turner. Bonds on the following: John Turner, Malacha Parmer, William Thompson, James Turner, William Harris, Jr., Samuel Harris, Richard Nowlin, Richard Sharp, James Farral, George Lackey and Richard Pilson.
Returned by the executor Adam Turner and John Tatum.
Jan Ct 1809.

Pgs 154-55   Date 16/18 Jan 1809
Item: Sales of the Estate of Jacob Adams, deceased made by Charles Foster and John Turner, executors. Sale consisting of household items, livestock and plantation tools to William Adams, James Keaton, John Reeves, Abraham Gossett, James Moles, Jesse Corn, Sr., Richard Sharp, George Lackey. Isaac Adams rented the plantation. Other sales to: Cornelius Keaton, John A. Corn, William Banks, Jr., Josiah Reeves, John Hall Sr., William Burnett, Samuel Harris, John Sharp jr., George Hairston, Jr., Lewis Foster, Joseph Reynolds, Robert Lockhart, John Glaspy, William Thompson, James Moles, Charles Foster, Jr, James Taylor, John Koger, James Ferrel, William Sharp, Sr, and Jr., and John James. Also, John Adams, Jr., William

Keaton Jr., Milly Corn, Barnard M. Price, Isaac Adams, John Harbour, John Sharp, Jr., Zachariah Keaton, Thomas Reeves, Mary Keaton, Abraham Reynolds, James Ferrell, Daniel McIntire and William Adams.
No total
Returned: Feb Ct 1809

Pg 155   Date: none
Land sold by the executors of the Estate of William Barton, deceased.
Four tracts of land sold and one rented.
Total: $1237.75
Returned: Feb Ct 1809

Pg 156   Date: none
List of articles sold at the Sale of the Robert Mayo Estate. To: Polly Mayo, Augustine Thomas, George Sprouse, William Gray, Edward Staples and Powell Gray. Cash received of Robert Mayo's wages at Norfolk.
No total or date

Pg 157   Date: 15 Jan 1809
William Deal Estate in Account with Soloman Keaton, Administrator.
Payments to: Mary S. S. Staples; trouble in attending Riggs Warrant, paid for having coffin made; paid George Lackey, paid Townly Riggs, paid for warrant and bringing back possessions in the hands of Noah Parr and others; paid for 1 gallon of brandy for the day of the sale; paid Richard Hopkins; paid Soloman Keaton; paid John Adams as a Commissioner; paid William Keaton for crying the property.
Total: 15.2.7
Returned: March Ct 1810

Pgs 158-159   Date: 6 Dec 1810
Estate of Isaac Adams deceased to Brett Stovall and William Adams, executors. Mentions: Thomas Adams, Leethy Adams, Joseph Adams, John Frans, Jr., William Adams, George Adams, David Perkins, John Sharp, Jr., Polly Adams, Leethy Adams, Joseph Adams, Thomas Adams are legatees. Also mentions Hardin Hairston, Capt. Gabriel Penn, Thomas Adams, Josiah Ferriss, John Hughes, Samuel Hughes.
Signed: Geo. Penn, W. Banks, Josiah Ferris, MartinMiller.
Returned: April Ct 1812.

Pg 159   Date: 25 Sept 1811
An account current of Leathey Adams deceased estate
agreeable to sales made by Maj. Brett Stovall, Adminis-
trator. To: Major William Carter, Gabriel Penn, Nathaniel
Smith. Mentions: William Adams, William Carter, Joseph
Adams. $139.75 to be divided between the legatees:
William Adams, Joseph Adams, Elisha Adams, Thomas Adams,
Polly Adams.
Signed: George Penn, William Banks, Martin Miller
Returned: April Ct 1812.

Pg 159   Date: 25 Sept 1811
An Account current of Hannah Adams' estate agreeable to
sales made by Brett Stovall.
Legatees: Elisha Adams, Polly Adams, William Adams,
Joseph Adams and Thomas Adams.
Signed: George Penn, William Banks, Martin Miller.
Returned: April Ct 1812.

Pgs 160-161   Date: 1814
An account of the estate of William Perkins deceased by
John Hall the acting Executor.
Taxes paid in Franklin County. Proportion made among
legatees of William Perkins: Christian Perkins, William
Perkins, David Perkins, Thomas Perkins, Sarah Reynolds,
Susannah Perkins, Nancy Boyd and Elizabeth Perkins.
Bonds on: Elizabeth Moss, Warren Massey, Benjamin Hick-
man, Thomas Perkins, James Cox, Susanah Perkins, Thomas
R. Hall, Col. George Hairston, John McAlexander, William
Burnett, Col. Samuel Hairston, John Shively, Joseph
Reynolds, Charles Thomas, Jr., Francis Wilks, Samuel
Saunder, James Cannaday, Nathan Cockram, Phillip Williams,
William Moore, Absalom Hancock, John Spaulden, William
Newberry, Ebenzer Watkins, Peter Guerrant, Elijah Dehart,
John Rakes, John Alexander, Reuben Harris and William Via.
Due the estate: 484.6.17
Each male legatees to receive: sixty four pounds, eight
shillings nine pence. Each female legatee: Fifty six
pounds twelve shillings and nine pence.
Signed: George Penn, Brett Stovall, Adam Turner, M.
Sandefur.
Returned: May Ct 1814.

Pg 162   Date: 1814
An account of the Estate of Robert Wright, deceased by
John Hall and Sarah Wright, executors.
Mentions: John Brammer, Sr., Reuben Short, John Hall,
Charles Thomas Jr., Joshua Adams, James McBride, James
Ingrum, Peter Saunders, William Sneed, Thomas Tennison,
Jesse Corn Jr., Charles Rakes, John Turner, Col. Peter
Saunders, Jesse Clark, Benjamin Nash and paid the Sheriff
of Buckingham County as per receipt.
Returned: May Ct 1814

Pgs 163-164   Date: 1803
An Account of the estate of Francis Turner, deceased by
Adam Turner, James Turner and John Turner, executors.
Balance due each Legatee $253.91
Paid taxes, paid Adam Turner for keeping Mother for three
years 3 moths $150.00.
Mentions: Richard Nowlin, John A. Corn, Washington Rowland,
Samuel Harris, Robert Rowan, Benet Houchins, Isham Harris,
William Pilson, Daniel Shealor, William Burnett.
Money lent to Robert Rowan by Elizabeth Turner.
Returned: Dec Ct 1816

Pg 164   Date: 24 March 1818
Settlement of the account with James Turner and his
father's estate (Francis Turner).
Signed: William Hancock, John Hall, John Sneed.

Pg 165   Date: 25 Oct 1817
Richard Thomas, Isaac Adams and John Sneed are appointed
to settle accounts of the estate of David Robertson,
deceased agreeable to his last Will and Testament, John
Conner the executor. The sum of $1,111.80 to be equally
divided between the following legatees: Milly Robertson,
John Conner, John Turner, David Robertson Jr., and
Sally Robertson, each to receive $222.36.
Returned: Nov Ct 1817.

Pg 166   Date: March 1818
Commissioners Jerman Baker, Warren Massey and James
Craddock to settle the account current of James Ingram
deceased. Part of the property appraised was willed to
James Ingrum and Paul C. Ingrum which is to be deducted.
Paid Francis Hail on personal occasion. Paid Alexander
Ingrum the executor.
Total: $1,849.37
Returned: Dec Ct 1818

Pg 167   Date: 1811-1816
Item: John E. Parr and Tahny (Thanny) Parr, infants of
John Parr, deceased, in account with Nathaniel Smith
their guardian. Mentions: John Tatum, John Webb, Gabriel
Penn, William Atkinson, William Lee, James Taylor, John
Askew, Joel Bundurant.
Total due wards: $765.52
Signed: M. Sandefur, Samuel Hanby, And. Joyce
Returned: Dec Ct 1816

Pg 168   Date: none
Estate of William Smith Sr., deceased in account with
John Smith, Executor.
Paid: Taxes; appraisers; William Joyce for making cofin:
Perren Cardwell, Joseph Gray, Samuel Corn, C. Standley,
John Webb; Nancy Parr as one of the legatees.
Total expenditure: $425.25
Returned: July Ct 1817

Pg 169   Date: 1816
Estate of William Smith in account with John Smith the
administrator.
Paid: P.R. Gilmer for attorney fees; Gabriel Penn for
spirits at the sale; Susannah Smith a legatee, in part;
George Rogers a legatee; Josiah S. Ellis a legatee;
William Thompson; William Moore; Perrin Cardwell; Daniel
Jones; Silas Carter; John Bohannon; Barnard Harris;
Christopher Stanley; Elijah Harris; William Smith; Harvey
Fitzgerald; William Carter; Nathaniel Smith; Samuel
Staples and John Harris for medicine. A note on
Bartholomew Smith; and cash in the hands of Munford Smith.
Total: $1,641.19
Returned: 21 June 1817

Pgs 170,171   Date: 2 July 1818
Estate of John Vancell, deceased in account with Elias
Vancil and John Vancil, Jr, administrators.
Land sold in Patrick County, Montgomery County and in
Kentucky. Other transactions with: Jonas Vancel, John
Weddle, William Carter, William Moore, Joseph Smith,
William Smith, Edmond Vancel, Munford Smith, William
Carter, Sr., Samuel Vancel, Adam Hall, W. Peake, Samuel
Staples, Arch. Whit, Samuel Hairston, John English,
Jonathan Elsick, Joseph Brim, Bart. Smith, James Smith,
Gilbert Bowman, Norman Bowman, Elisha Ayres William
Sawers, Robert Strange, AAron Bowman, Jonathan Landrith,

David P. Simon, John Fry.
Total: $4,455.97
Returned: Dec Ct 1818

Pg 171   Date: 13 Oct 1819
David Hudson part that Jacob Hudson His guardian,
received from Hill Hudson's estate, the sum being
$488.87.
Dated: 14 Jan 1818. Signed: William Booker, John Tatum,
Samuel Flippen.
Returned: Sept Ct 1819.

Pgs 172-177   Date: 5-16 May 1817
Sales of the estate of John Vancel, Sr., deceased.
Included: livestock, smith tools, traps, household
furniture, kitchen utensils, gun, wool, bee hives,
plantation tools, tract of land called "the Green Tract"
tracts called Hall and Pennington tracts.
Sales to: Elias Vancel, John Vancel, George Smith,
William Carter, Jr., Richard Herring, Nicholas Marroy,
Charles Bolt Jr., Peter Beller, John Epperson, Joseph
V. Grigg, Bartlett Smith, Thomas Dillard, William Carter,
Sr., James Dillard, James Bays, Benjamin Landreth, William
McCraw, William McPeak, Joseph Smith, William Hanby,
Samuel Hanby, Jonathan Landreth, Elisha Bellar, Johnson
Snow, William McMillion, Hayman Bowman, Samuel Camron,
John Webb, George Smith, Gilbert Bowman, John Oneal,
Robert Wilson.
No total
Returned: April Ct 1818

Pg 178   Date: 13 May 1814
List of debts due the estate of William Perkins, deceased.
..Elizabeth Moss, Benjamin Hickman, Thomas Perkins, James
Cox, Susannah Perkins, Thomas R. Hall, Col. George Hairs-
ton, John McAlexander, William Burnett, Col. Samuel
Hairston, Phillip Williams, William Moore, Absalom Hancock,
John Spalden, William Newberry, Ebenezer Watkins, Peter
Garren, Elijah Dehart, Charles Rakes, Rueben Harris, John
Shively, Joseph Reynolds, Charles Thomas, Jr., Francis
Wilks, Samuel Saunders, James Canaday, Nathan Cocram,
William Vier, William Boyd, Elisha Rakes, Adam Turner,
John Hall, Pleasant Thomas, Warren Massey.
The sale of Joseph Reynolds land is not stated.
                                        John Hall
Total: L517.2.4
Returned: May Ct 1814

Pgs 179-181   Date: 8 Jan 1816
Amount of sales of property of William Smith, Jr., deceased.
Sales to: George Rogers, Isham Cook, John Fields, Joseph Sharp, William Hanby, John Epperson, James Fulkerson, William Sharp, Nathaniel Smith, Benjamin Carrel, John Halbert, John Webb, George Leaman, Cornelius Hart, John Smith, William Keaton, Robert Hairston, John Hughes, John Harris, Gabriel Penn, William Helm, Harden Hairston, Jesse Murphy, Thomas Helm, Bernard Harris, Clement Vawler?, Francis T. Gaines, John Tatum, Edward Collings, William Collings, Daniel Collings, Richard Beasley, Joseph Gray, Gilbert Bowman, William Burge, Daniel Martindale, Pendleton Gains, Charles Wilson, Obediah Wilson, John Askew, William Martindale, Joel Lee, John Webb, Reuben Wats, Christopher Stanley, Melkijah Frans, Elijah Harris, James Owen, John Cardwell, Thurston Gains.
Includes: Household furniture, guns, blowing horn, hay, corn, cattle, steers, a watch, desk, horses, shoe tools, books, pewter, flax wheel, sheep, hogs, also 225 acres and 762 acres of land sold to Nathaniel Smith.
No total
Returned: Nov Ct 1819

Pg 181   Date: 31 May 1820
An Account of the Estate of John Johnson, deceased.
Charles Lewis and Jane Johnson administrators.
Property sales 16 Jan 1819   420.93
Accts against the Estate   191.08
John Gwin for cost   3.00
Pd. Martin Johnson   29.00
Signed: Thomas Whitlock, Jesse Mankin, Jacob Grigg.
Returned: July Ct 1820

Pg 182   Date: 5 Nov 1819
Estate of William Smith, Jr., deceased, John Smith, administrator.
Expenditures and credits:
Nathaniel Smith as curator of said estate for services.
Clks ticket - Montgomery County
Williamson Smith, Gabriel Penn, Samuel Staples, M. Sandefur, Richard Thomas, Floyed Webb, Jackson Smith, Cash Tatum, Mary Parr, Juball & Strange, Printers in Lynchburg, Horatio Penn, James D. Garland fee for Tatum and wife, John Smith for his trouble in suit against Tatum and wife. P. R. Gilmore fee against Beazley.
No Total
Returned: Nov Ct 1819

Pg 183   Date: 16 Nov 1820
Account of Madison Moore Estate of Madison and
William Moore by their guardian William Carter, Jr.
No total
Returned: Nov Ct 1820

Pg 183   Date: 16 Nov 1820
Gallehue Moore guardian for Hardin Moore, Samuel
Moore, Alfred Moore and John Moore.
Inventory as of 19 July 1819 - $1,776.96
Returned: Nov Ct 1820

Pg 184   Date: 30 June 1820
Property sold of the estate of Milly Robertson,
deceased, widow of David Robertson, deceased.
Includes: Furniture, pewter, Bible, books, tables,
kitchen item, farming equipment and livestock.
Sales to: Elijah Dehart, Rachel Davis, John Elgin,
Gabriel Bolling, Mrs Nancy Hubbard, William McAlexander,
Jesse Dehart, William Canaday, Benjamin Hubbard, John
Hubbard, Jonathan Hubbard, Jesse Hubbard, William Conner,
Marvill Bolling, Samuel Harris, Arthur Garvin, Richard
Hopkins, Crawford. Burnett, Prior Pendleton.
Total: $230.66
Returned: Oct Ct 1820

Pg 185   Date: 30 Oct 1819
The Estate of Thomas Ayres, deceased.
Property and land sold.
Payments made to: Elcany Ayres, James Dickerson, William
Carter, Martin Cloud, Jacob Grigg, Jesse Mankin,
Samuel Hanby.
Total: $697.81
Returned: June Ct 1820

Pg 186   Date: 9 Dec 1820
Estate of Benjamin Terry, deceased in account with
Obediah Burnett.
By sales   222.32
Expenditures for the family
for yrs 1817-1819   60.00
Pd Elijah Harris, one of the
legatees who md Viny Terry   20.59
Pd. Nancy Terry   10.00

Distributed among the legatees each to receive $23.19.
Viney Terry wife of Elijah Harris received $20.59;
Nancy Terry $10.00; Others are: Samuel, John, Sally,
Polly and Benjamin to receive a full share which
remains in the hands of Obediah Burnett their guardian.
Returned: Dec Ct 1820

Pg 187   Date: 11 Jan 1821
Inventory of the property and money in many hands in
1819 by Gabriel Hanby, guardian for Patience Jane
Moore, infant.
Cash: $444.22, for hire of three negros $81.00,
Total: $525.22
Returned: Jan Ct 1821

Pgs 187-188   Date: 8 June 1821
Account current of James Carter deceased, according to
sales of land, negros and other dealings for a total
of $2,016.78.
Sales to: George Carter for 130 acres of land; Silas
Carter, Abram. Staples, Daniel Mitchell, John B. Hudson,
William Sharp, Daniel Witt, George C. Dodson, Munford
Smith, William Carter, Jr., William Clark, Samuel Nowlin,
William Carter, Sr., Murphy Ayres, Mathew Sandefer,
Farthing Hix, Philpenia Sharp, Frederick Critz,
Hamon Critz Sr., Claiborne Shelton, John Franx, Harvey
Fitzgerald.
Among the items sold: household furniture, cattle,
negros, a prompter's book, a dicktionary, a Columbian
orator.
Expenditures:
William Lyon as singing master
Stephen Hubbard for preaching funeral
P. R. Gilmore for legal advise
Obediah Belcher for making the coffin
Samuel Howell, as an appraiser
Richard Herring for store account
S. Staples - account
William Lyon as cryer
George Carter, administrator of the estate
William Clark.
Returned: June Ct 1821

Pg 189   Date: 20 March 1821
Madison Moore to William Carter, guardian.
An accounting for the year 1819-1820.
Clothing paid Joshua W. Garrett for making a hat,
Paid for book, paid Joseph W. Grigg for three months
schooling and board; paid Major Carter for nine months
schooling and board; paid Burwell Smith's wife for making a coat.
Total expenditure: $50.62
Returned: July Ct 1821

Pg 190   Date: 20 March 1821
William Carter, Jr., guardian for William H. Moore for
part of the year 1819 and 1820.
Expenditures:

3 pr pantallons, buttons & making	3.00
3 pr cotton pantaloons, etc	2.00
5 shirts cotten, buttons & making	5.15
4 pr stockings	1.50
4 pr shoes	3.00
1 wool hat	.75
Paid J.W. Garrett for making hat	.50
1 yarn coat	1.25
1 Black Burnbasette Coat	1.75
1 Spelling book	.25
Pd Joseph V. Griggs for 3 months schooling	1.50
same for 3 months board	7.50
Pd Maj. Carter 9 months schooling	6.00
same board for 9 months	22.50
Pd Burwell Smith's wife for making coat	.50
	$ 57.25

Returned: July Ct 1821

Pg 191
Surveyed 27 Nov 1821 for Samuel Moore, 299 acres of
land, it being his part of his father's land on Mill
Creek, crosses Ararat River, survey made by John Creed.
Signed: Brett Stovall, SPC

Pg 191
26 Nov 1821 surveyed land for Lethea Moore, 509 acres
it being her part of her father's land.

Pg 191   Date: 27 Nov 1821
Survey for Madison Moore, 525 acres, it being his part
of his father's land, adjoining Munford Smith, Bartlett
Smith and the Pennington line.

Pg 191   Date: 28 Nov 1821
Survey for John Moore 462 acres of land it being his
part of his father's land.

Pg 192   Date: 12 Sept 1822
Legislature of North Carolina of 1820 appoint a
Commission to settle the estate with Virginia of the
heirs of William Moore, deceased.
To: Hardin H. Moore, son of William Moore, land in
Surry County, North Carolina 500 acres on Pauls Creek,
the Chamberlain tract of 222 acres in Patrick County
from Bingham also 100 acres recorded from same.
To: William Carter and Elizabeth Carter, his wife and
daughter and heir of William Moore deceased, the Lower
lot of the Armstrong place containing 326 acres agreeable to Pla.t in Surry Co. N.C.
To Samuel Moore, son and heir, the second lot of the
house tract containing 299 acres in the County of
Patrick; 400 acres in the County of Grayson on the
waters of Read Island patent in the name of John Bolt
and William Garrett.
To Alfred Moore, son and heir, the middle lot of the
Armstrong place containing 285 acres in Surry Co. NC
To John Moore, son and heir, the lower lot of the home
tract containing 462 acres in Patrick County, also
400 acres on Johnson Creek in Patrick County.
To Leathea R. Moore, daughter and heir, the two lots
of the home tract containing 509 acres and 50 acres
from David Rowark and 50 acres from Elizabeth Williams.
To Madison T. Moore, son and heir, 525 acres in Patrick
County.
To William Moore, son and heir, one tract in Surry Co.
NC on the middle fork of the Arrarat River known as
the McKinley tract; also 452 acres in Grayson Co from
Thomas Hunt, also 228 acres recorded in same name.
To Palina Jane Moore (Patience) daughter and heir, the
upper lot of the Armstrong tract contains 240 acres in
Surry Co. NC, 400 acres in Patrick County by deed from
McCraw's executors.
Signed: J. Tatum, Samuel Flippen, William Carter,
John Whitlock, Elijah Harris, Mallory Smith.
Returned: Oct Ct 1822

Pg 193   Date: 30 Jan 1821
A list of all money paid Jeremiah Baker and Chesley
Ashlin, administrators of the estate of Jerman Baker,
deceased.
To: Jeremiah Baker; David Custer for making coffin;
Daniel Stone; John Pace; John Lenox; E. Boulden;
H. Clabour for attorney fees; Greensville Penn;
Dr. L. P. Stovall; Constable Wooten; Peter Smith;
Spencer James; Martha Greenlee; John Hughes; John C.
Traylor; John Dillard an administrator.
Total: $4,758.10
Signed: Thomas Penn; Carrington Dillion, Joseph Kenn-
erly.
Returned: March Ct 1822

Pgs 194-96   Date: 15 Sept 1821
An Account of sales of the estate of Peter Scales,
deceased.
Sold: Sheep, wagon, wheat at the Mill, salt, cattle,
horses, a silver watch, household furniture, money
scales, razors and cases, distillery, blacksmith
tools, rent of the Mill, books, kitchen utensils.
Sales to: Phillip Anglin, Stephen Atkinson, John
Burress, Levi Clinkscales, Gabriel Critze, Lambert
Dodson, James Gibson, John Hughes, Joseph Hutcheson,
James Harris, Richard Jones, David Kallam, William
Moore, Andrew Martin, John Martin, Oney Scales,
John Scales, Edward C. Staples, Edward Tilley,
Daniel Hitt, Jesse Young.
No Total
Returned by: P.D. Scales and Nathaniel Scales,
administrators.

Pgs 197-200   Date: 19 Nov 1821 and
                                31 Dec 1821
An account of sales of the estate of Peter Scales,
deceased. Sales of: Wheat, blacksmith tools, window
glass, loom, furniture, horses, salt, cattle, saddles,
saddle bags, tobacco, flax wheel, rent of distillery
and mill for one year to Peter Leak also Bufflow land;
oil mill pond and rent of Nathan Goings place; flour,
rent of negros, baskets, rocking cradle.
No total
Returned: Feb Court 1822

Pg 200   Date: 22 Nov 1823
Estate of Thomas Dillard in account with William Carter,
administrator from 1820-1823.
Paid: Mary Cox one of the legatees, in full
Paid: James Dillard one of the legatees in part
Paid: William McMillin one of the legatees on account
Paid: Edward Dillard one of the legatees on account
Paid: Thomas and Joseph Smith, appraisers
Paid: Joseph V. Grigg for crying property at the sale
Paid: John Branson, one of the legatees in full
Paid: John Bolt one of the legatees in full
Paid: Ruth McMillion the amount of her account
Paid: Dabney Walker note
Total: $2,417.59
Signed: M. Sandefur, Samuel Hanby Jr., John Tatum
Returned: Dec Ct 1823

Pg 201   Date: 11 Nov 1823
Account of money paid by Jeremiah Baker and Cheslin
Ashlin on account of Jereman Baker, deceased.
Paid: Clerks ticket from Henry County
Paid Sheriff of Henry County
Paid Clerk of Patrick County
John Carter, Nathaniel H. Claiborne, Pechey R. Gilmore,
G.W. Turner, Spencer James and Clerk of Franklin County.
Total: $1,011.71
Returned: Nov Ct 1823

Pg 201   Date: 6 March 1822
Alfred Moore account with G. Moore, guardian from Dec
1820 to Dec 1822
Paid out:
1 pr lain shoes	1.25
Waistcoat & making	3.05
Makeing panteloons	.57
2 cotton shirts	3.50
2 pr panteloons	2.37
1 pr fine shoes	4.37
1 pr liney panteloons	1.12
1 pr woolen socks	.40
5 yds twill cloth	3.00
making coat	1.25
making 1 pr twill panteloons	.50
Schooling	6.50
12 months boarding	35.00
	$62.90

Commissioners: Joseph Smith, Thomas Whitlock, Jacob
Griggs.
Returned: March Ct 1823

Pg 202   Date: June-Aug 1821
Samuel Moore ward of G. Moore in account with
Perkins and Walker. Paid for socks, waistcoat, stockings,
nankeen, paper, wine, castor oil
Total: $20.58

                          Date: Dec 1820 to
                                Aug 1821
Samuel Moore in account with G. Moore.
Saddle, panteloons, jacket, shirts, shoes, boarding
and schooling.
Total: $76.52
Returned: March Ct 1823

Pg 203   Date: 6 March 1822
John Moore, ward of G. Moore, an account from Dec 1820
to Dec 1821.
Shoes, shirt, panteloons, coat, socks, materials,
schooling and boarding, a total of $58.05.
Returned: March Ct 1823

Pg 203   no date
Galiheu Moore, guardian for Samuel Moore, Alfred Moore
and John Moore reports for year 1821.
To hire of negros $132.00
Returned: March Ct 1823

Pgs 204-205   Date: 31 Oct 1823
Sales of remaining balance of the estate of William Smith
Sr., deceased.
Sold: furniture, ox cart, blacksmith tools, books, pewter,
livestock.. Sales to: Daniel Coalson, Christopher Stanley,
Josiah Rogers, Alexander Joyce, Munford Smith, Williamson
Smith, Floyd Webb, Levi Clinkscales, Clifton Keaton,
James Lyon, William Blansett, Thomas Fitzgerald, Capt.
George Carter, Capt. John Tatum, John Duvall, Jeremiah
Wood, Clark Penn, Francis Nowlin, John Richman, Samuel
Gilbert, Elijah Gray, Samuel Fodrell, Robert Boaz.
Not totaled
Returned: Dec Ct 1823 by John Smith, executor

Pgs 206-207   Date: July 1819-Dec 1822
Leathey R. Moore in account with William McCraw her guardian
expenses - no total.
Shoes, silk, cotton cloth, pd: Johnathan Unthank(Unthank)
paid Booth for schooling, Dr. B. Franklin, John Whitlock,
William Slade, straw bonnet, damask, flannel, shawl,
bombazene material, side combs, ribbons, paper, pins, cal-
lico, morocco shoes, tuck combs, gingham, muslin, cambrick,

Robert Terry account, silk shawl, slippers, lace, skeins of silk, mull muslin, note to William Carter for William H. Mooore, note to G. Moore for Samuel Moore, John Martin, Thomas Tune, Acheles Detheridge.
Balance: $1,166.24
Leathy R. Moore one of the infants of William Moore, deceased.
Returned: Dec Ct 1823

Pg 208   Date: 1821-22
William H. Moore in account with William Carter, his guardian. Paid: Clothing, board, Dr. Franklin for medicine; paid Gallihu Moore, John Moore, Madison Moore, Leathey R. Moore, Gabriel Hanby, William McCraw, Palina J. (Patience) Moore, Alfred Moore, H.H. Moore.
Expenses: $ 87.06.   Income: $985.67
Returned: Dec Ct 1823

Pg 209   Date: 8 Sept 1823
Madison T. Moore in account with William Carter, his guardian, account for 1821 and 1822. Paid for clothing boarding, amount due William H. Moore and Leathy R. Moore.
Credit - rent of land to Hardin H. Moore.
No Total - Returned: Dec Ct 1823

Pg 210   Date: 11 Sept 1823
Samuel Moore in account with Galliheu Moore, his guardian for 1822. Paid, my mother for clothing furnished, for schooling and board in Tennessee to Claren Moore; clothing and Dr. Loving.
Expenses: $96.39   Income: $333.25
Returned: Dec Ct 1823

Pg 211   Date: 10 Sept 1823
Account of John Moore, infant of William Moore deceased, with Galliheu Moore his guardian.
Paid: for clothing, boarding, Patterson the schoolmaster, William Carter and William H. Moore.
Expenses: $93.67   Income: $137.00
Returned: DecCt 1823

Pg 212   Date: 10 Sept 1823
Alfred Moore in account with Galliheu Moore, his guardian. Paid for clothing, for splitting and putting up 1350 rails, board at Scales in Rockingham for six months. William Herring; paid William Carter, paid William H.

Moore, paid for schooling.
Expenses: $189.00   Income: $96.50
Returned: Dec Ct 1823

Pg 213   Date: 25 Aug 1823
Estate of James Ingrum in account with Alexander and
Martha Ingrum, executors.
Paid: Mary Ingrum one of the legatees
Paid: Jesse Corn, Charles Foster, M. Sandefur
Returned: Dec Ct 1823

Pg 213   Date: 31 March 1824
Account current of administrators of Jermin Baker,
deceased. John P. Hill, expense, $142.67.
Signed: Edward Philpott, Jesse Corn, John Koger Jr.,
Charles Foster Jr.
Returned: June Ct 1824

Pgs 214-215   Date: 24 Nov 1824
Estate of James Bartlett Sr., deceased in account with
the executors. John Massey is guardian of Ann C. Bartlett
and Nancy G. Bartlett.
Legatees: John Massey, Warren Massey and James Bartlett.
Paid: Marvil Bowling, Costilo Hill, Thomas Boling, Fanny
Wood, Reuben Short, Francis Howell, Samuel Saunders,
Richard Thomas, John Hall, Jesse Corn, William Canaday,
Fleming Hall, William Ayres, Jeremiah Burnett, Jefferson
Taylor, Nathaniel Akers, Thomas Tennison, Jesse Dehart,
William Martin, Stephen Hubbard, Edmund Bartlett, Thomas
Sneed, George Washington. Land in Floyd County, Kentucky.
Balance due estate $272.12
Returned: Dec Ct 1824

Pg 215   Date: 4 Nov 1824
Estate of William Smith, Senr. deceased in account with
John Smith.
Paid Legatees: Susannah Smith, Bartholomew Smith, Harbart
Smith, Nathaniel Smith, Daniel Franse, Jane Lyon, Henry
Smith, I..h S. Ellis, Isum Smith, Mark Smith, Thomas
Stanley, Sindy Stanley and paid Nancy Parr per order.
Total paid: $360.26
Returned: Nov Ct 1824

Pg 216
Inquistion taken on the Meadow branch in the woods in
the County of Patrick 7 Oct 1824 before Samuel Martin,

Coroner, to view the body of a negro man, name unknown, lying dead and upon oaths of Asa Ballard, Lemuel Joyce, William Joyce Jr., James Joice and Joseph Martin, men of Stokes County, North Carolina, to determine what manner said man met his death. One Edward P. Williams late of Stokes Co. NC, in the county of Patrick, not having God before his eyes, but being moved and seduced by the instigation of the devil, did shoot and mortally wound said unknown man. Edward Parker Williams did kill, murder against the peace and dignity of the Commonwealth. John Hughes, foreman, Clark Penn, M. R. Hughes, C. J. Ferrell, James Fulkerson, Abram Penn, Brett Stovall, Reuben Hughes, Stephen Atkinson, John Poindexter, Edward Thomas, Frederick Critz.

Pg 217   Date: 26 Aug 1823
Estate of William Smith, Jr., deceased in account with John Smith, administrator.
Paid John Tatum. William Smith, Sr., heir at large of the descedent. William Clark. Expenses to Lynchburg after Basinger debt; to Clements on same business.
Mentions: Mary Parr, Bartholomew Smith, Nathaniel Smith, Isham Smith, John Hughes, Williamson Smith.
Total of estate: $5,582.52
Returned: June Ct 1824

Pg 218   Date: 28 Jan 1824
Pelina J. Moore in account with Gabriel Hanby her guardian, years 1819-1821. Board, William Carter, Jr., spelling books. Micheaux for schooling. William McCraw, Galihue Moore, W. Low for schooling. Expense: $882.24
Income: $878.39
Returned: Aug Ct 1824

Pg 219   Date: 1823-24
Estate of Richard L. Whitlock, deceased in account with John P. Carter, administrator. Paid: George Hairston, William Via, Warren Massey, Barnard M. Price.
Total: $ 60.28
Returned: June Ct 1824

Pg 220-221   Date: April 1825
Estate of John Tuggle, Sr., deceased in account with R. Thomas and William Hancock, executors.
Paid: Robert Cook, Payton Gravely, Adam Turner, William Brammer, William Lee, John Tuggle, Jesse Jones,

Gabriel Bolling, Jacob Sheler, Jefferson Taylor,
Costilo Hill, Fleming Hall, Isaac Adams, James Tuggle,
E. Dehart, Brett Stovall, Samuel Saunders, Sheriff
of Patrick; James Via, Dandridge Slaughter, M. Sandefur,
Robert Craig, John Anderson, Richard Wells, James
Tuggle, Jesse Jones, Samuel Staples, Nathan Hall,
Thomas Bolling, William Lyon, Samuel Harris, Arthur
Garvan, Edward Parmer, William Burnett.
Paid Legatees: Reuben Burnett, Henry Tuggle and Shadrack
Brammer.
Signed: M. Sandefur, William Ayres, Isaac Adams
Balance due after expenses: $1,218.68
Returned: Aug Ct 1825

Pg 221   Date: 1 Jan 1824
Account current of Gallehue Moore guardian for John
Moore.
Expenses: Land tax, clothing, board and tuition at
Madison Academy $60.50, cash, a Latin dictionary.
Expenses: $93.65 Income: $168.25
Signed: Thomas Whitlock, Arch. Stuart, Joseph Smith
Returned: May Ct 1825

Pg 222   Date: 11 May 1825
Estate of Richard Harrison, deceased in account with
F. B. Harrison, administrator (Francis B. Harrison).
Paid: M. Sandefur, William Ayres, John Wills, A. Staples,
John Hughes, William Lyon, tavern bill in Lynchburg.
Signed: J.G. Lee, William Critz, H. Critz
Returned: May Ct 1825

Pg 223   Date: 14 Nov 1824
Account current of G. Moore guardian for Alfred C. Moore.
Clothing, cash, D. Walker, W. Fleming for making shoes,
board and tuition at Madison Academy, paid William Slade,
1 copy of Horace, Cicero, Caesar, one Greek Testament.
Expenses: $138.29 Income: $146.30
Returned: May Ct 1825

Pg 224   Date: 14 Nov 1824
Account current of Galiheu Moore guardian for Sameul Moore
Paid: S. Hickerson, William McCraw, tuition and board at
Madison Academy. Expense: $190.03 Income: $105.00
Returned: May Ct 1825

Pg 225   Date: 6 Dec 1824
Estate of Lemuel Hix, deceased in account with Dudley McMillian.
Expenses: Paid William Nowland, Jr., John Boyd, John A. Cloud, John Hix, William Bayles Jr., Jesse Mankin for making a coffin, Josiah Heath, Joshua Haynes, Martin Cloud, William Ayres.
Total: $117.66
Returned: Feb Ct 1825

Pg 226   Date: 12 May 1825
Sales of property of Ben. Philpott deceased by A. Staples.
To: Capt. Ayres, John Philpott, William Edwards.
Includes: furniture, books, a horse. Total: $59.56
Returned: June Ct 1825

Pgs 227-230   Date: 15 Dec 1825
William Moore deceased in account with William Carter, administrator. Payments: Galihue Moore an heir, William Carter an heir; Gabriel Hanby, Jane Moore an heir, William McCraw, Letha Moore an heir, Samuel Moore an heir, John Moore an heir, William H. Moore an heir, Madison T. Moore an heir, S. McKiney, Elijah Harris, John Tatum, Samuel Flippen, William Carter, Sr., John Whitlock, William Sawyers, Drury East for spirits at sale in Grayson Co., Joseph Jessup Sr., John Bingham, Anthony Going, Joseph V. Grigg, James Tate, John Sprager for making coffin, John C. Traylor for preaching funeral service, William East, Adam Hale, Nathaniel Scales for boarding boys, John Eaton, John Bowman Jr., Joseph Pike, Peachy R. Gilmer, William Reynolds, William McCraw Jr., Edward Jones, Greensville Willis, Zadock Hale, Thomas Snow, John Hix, Robert Daniel, Widow Landrith, Early Ennis, Isham Puckett, Lemuel Ayres, Dudley McMillion William Reynolds Sr., Nathaniel Reynolds, William Smith, Benjamin Going, Peter Beller, Stephen McKinney, Charles Bolt, Samuel Staples, James McCraw, Levi Jones, Samuel Smith for schooling, Thomas Baldwin, Munford Smith, Richard Snow, Joseph Draper, Johnson Reynolds, Jesse Brown, Elijah Jessup, Jacob Horton, Hamon Bowman, Robert Harris, Elihu Ayres, Elkannah Ayres, Leonard Owen, Aaron Bowman, Bartlett Smith, David Pearce, George Smith, John Hamacker, William Golding, Hale Snow, Edward Jones, James Edwards, Joseph Pike, Benjamin Reynolds, Philip Anglin, Beverly Bays, William Bays, William Tifton, John Hammaker, Henry Hines, Samuel McCleern, William Ballard Jr and Sr., Reuben Branscomb, James Branscomb, Abram Hawks, John Hawks, Jacob Hudson, Martin Walker, James Tate, Benjamin B. Landrith, William Clark

John W. Burch, James Howell, Leonard Bowman, Nicholas Murray, Baines Ahart, Adam Ahart, William Going Sr., Ice Snow, Isham Barrett, Sukey Hensley, Maj. Wm. Carter, Joseph Brim, William Grigg, Shadrack Roberts, John B. Walker, Jonathan Landrith, Nathaniel C. Young, Thomas Going, Jarrel Tate, John Pucket, Adam Hall, John W. Sparger, David Pierce, John Scott, Elisha Edwards, Burwell Smith, William Hanby.
John Dalton rent of Hunt place. Adam Hall rent of Poplar Cove Creek place.
Paid: $7,773.74, Cash and Bonds $8,207.19, Bal: $428.44
Commissioners: John Tatum, Samuel Flippen, Arch. Stuart.

Pg 231   Date: --
Estate of William Moore in account with William Carter administrator.
Expense going from Petersburg to Richmond to get right of land; sale at Grayon County, attending Surry Court, going to Poplar Camp to settle with David Pearce, same at White Plains; same at Beasleys. James and Hiram Bolt of Grayson County.
Total: $244.50
Returned: Dec Ct 1825

Pgs 232-235   Date: 28 March 1825
Property of Jesse Young sold --Sales to:
John Pollard, James Joyce, Mary Carter, West Lankford, Sarah Young widow, James Young, William Grey, John Joyce, Tandy Hollandsworth, William Moore, John Smith, Stephen Poor, Edward Tilly, John Standly, Richard C. Ally, George Harrison, Benjamin Frasure, Daniel Grey, William Joyce Sr., William Cannon, Thomas Joyce Jr., Peter Critz, Enoch Bardale, Elizabeth Williams, Elijah Grey, Eleven??Grey, Joseph Smith, Jesse Radford, William C. Joyce, Joseph Martin, William Keaton, Abraham Frasure, Hugh Poor, Lemuel Joyce, John Webb, Asa Ballard, Thomas Hudwell, Daniel Hollandsworth, Mary Hollandsworth, Samuel Martin, William T. Joyce, David Wray, Martha Stephens, Brett Stovall, Lewis Turner, John Iron, William Nelson 3 qts brandy purchased by a Club.
Items sold: plantation tools, pewter, geese, potatoes, horse, family Bible, one tin trumpet, furniture, hogs, kitchen utensils, cattle. No total
Returned: May Ct 1826

Pg 236   Date: 18 March 1826
Account current of Ignatious Simms, deceased.
Samuel Saunders, paid taxes Patrick & Franklin Cos, Jerman Baker, Thomas Carter. Signed: John Parker, Charles Foster, Jr.
Total: $832.35   Returned: March Ct 1826

Pgs 237-238   Date: none
Sale of property of Richard Stone, deceased to:
David Dyer, Martha Stone, John Stone, Aaron Lee, Stephen Stone, Carrington Dillion, Tandy Stone, Washington L. Bailey, John Franklin, James Dyer, Peter Young, Joseph Mayner, Samuel Smith.
Consists of: household items, side saddle, cattle, hogs, books, Bible, hymn book, looking glass, gun, horses.
Returned: May Ct 1825

Pg 238   Date: none
Sale of Micajah Stone's property to:
John Carter, Jacob Prillaman, George Prillaman, Baily Martin, John Stone, Charles Massey, Peter Davis, Samuel Smith, Samuel H. Ferguson, William Standly, James Lesueurs, William Davis, Ezekiel Jones. Includes: Saddle, bee hives, hogs, corn, bacon.
Returned: Dec Ct 1825   No total
The within list of sales of the property of Micajah Stone a lunatic in the hospital at Williamsburg.

Pgs 239-241   Date: 4 Aug 1825
Sale of property of Richard Stone, deceased by John Stone, administrator. Sales to: Tandy Stone, Stephen Stone, John Stone, Patsy Stone, Esibeah Stone, Elizabeth Stone, William Standly, Lewis Foster, Hutson Akers, John W. Philpott, Hampton Haynes, Washington L. Bayley, Samuel H. Ferguson, Peter Young, John Syms, James Lesuer, David Dyer, Tarleton King, William Wray, John Bell, William Spencer, James Turner, William Turner, Benjamin Davis, Jacob Prillaman, Obediah Turner, William Davis, John Hunter, William Via, Aaron Noe, Adam Noe, John Payne, Meshack Turner, William Draper, Peter David, Peter Smith, Chendle Law, Pines Allen, Booker Mullins, John Whooten, Peter Smith, Thomas Sharp, Obadiah Hunt, Jeremiah Baker, Lewis Foster.
Includes: plantation tools, saddles, household furniture, tobacco, corn, cattle, sheep, hogs, horses.
Returned: May Ct 1826

Pgs 241-242   Date: none
Appraisal of the estate of Richard Tucker Mayner, deceased by Joseph Cummings, John Medley, Ignatious Sims.
Includes: household items, saddle, farming equipment, horse, books, cattle. Total: ₤ 108.6.9
Returned: Jan Ct 1799

Pg 242   Date: 1 Feb 1808
Inventory of the estate of Hannah Adams, deceased.
One bay mare and cold, one bed and furniture, one
womans saddle. Total: $18.15. Appraisers: Richard
Harrison, Josiah Ferris, Jacob Critz, John Frans.
Returned: March Ct 1808

Pg 243   Date: 5 Dec 1806
Inventory of the estate of Mark Parr, deceased.
Furniture, horses, books. Total: $375.29
Signed: Gabriel Penn, Robert Sharp, M. Sandefur
Returned: Dec Ct 1806

Pg 243   Date: 15 Jan 1808
Inventory estate of Jacob Adams by Benjamin Hancock,
Thomas Reeves, David Harbour.
Eight negros, horses, sheep, furniture, cattle,
kitchen items. Total: L 845.4.9
Returned: Feb Ct 1808

Pgs 244-245   Date: 5 Dec 1806
Inventory of the estate of John Parr, Jr., deceased.
Farm animals, horses, plantation equipment, guns,
furniture, wagons, a still, blacksmith tools, five
negros. By: Nathaniel Smith, Jesse Tatum, Gabriel
Penn, M. Sandefur, Robert Sharp.
Returned: Dec Ct 1806

Pg 245
Inventory of the estate of Leathy Adams, deceased.
Horse, household items, negro.
By: W. Banks, E. Banks, Martin Miller, Joseph Stovall
Total: $134.33
Returned: Sept Ct 1809

Pg 246   Date: 11 Feb 1808
Moveable estate of William Barton, deceased.
Cattle, plantation equipment, kitchen furniture, furni-
ture, horses, Bible, one book "Confession of Faith",
two other books, hymn book and "Pilgrim's Progress".
By: William Jones   Total L 63.10.3

Pg 247   Date: 24 March 1808
Inventory estate of James Goins, deceased..horses, hogs,
furniture, guns cattle. By Peter Beller, John Strange,
Charles Bolt.   Total $520.69
Returned: April Ct 1808

Pgs 248-249   Date: 9 Apr 1808
Inventory estate of John Parr, Sr., Includes: hogs, horses, horse cart, plantation equipment, shoe makers tools, kitchen equipment, gun, shot bag and powder horn, Testament, a parcel of old books, spice mortor, money scales, furniture. By: Samuel Clark, Samuel Corn, George Clark. No total
Returned: May Ct 1808

Pg 249   Date: 25 May 1808
Inventory estate of Thomas Hornsby deceased. Horses, furniture, cattle, tools, books, 2 negros. By Nathaniel Smith, Elijah Collings, Andrew Joyce.
Total: $573.41

Pg 250   Date: Sept 1808
Inventory estate of William Deal deceased. Household items, gun, saddle, flax wheels, cotton wheale. By David Taylor, John Adams, John James
No total
Returned: Dec Ct 1808

Pg 251   Date: 1 Aug 1809
Inventory estate of Robert Wright deceased by William Sneed, William Fuson, Jesse Clark. Gun, flax wheel, kitchen articles, furniture, six negros, horses, a bond on Henry Deshazo and William Banks.
Total: L 324.5.9
Returned: Oct 1809

Pg 252   Date: 10 Feb 1809
A further inventory of the estate of Jacob Adams, deceased. Livestock, bee hives, oats, rye, corn, a bond on John Mankin, George Lackey, John Akers, James Turner, account of Thomas Bowling, John Turner Sr., Lewis Ross, Thomas Reeves, Benjamin Hancock, William Adams. By: Thomas Reeves, Benjamin Hancock, David Harbour.
Returned: April Ct 1809

Pgs 253-254   Date: not stated
Inventory estate of W.B.(Beveridge) Hughes, deceased. Livestock, horses, two negros, furniture, hunting saddle, mans saddle, tools, rifle gun, books, pewter. Credits: Benjamin Mayo, William Burnett, Robert Lockhart, Malachi Parmer, Richardson Mayo, George Corn, William Balisle, John A. Hancock. Appraisers: David Harbour, William Hancock, John Turner. Total:L1170.26.0

Pgs 255-262   Date: 17 April 1809
Inventory taken of the estate of Jesse Corn, deceased,
by Charles Foster, John Burnett, William Fuson, Thomas,
Reaves, John Hall. Includes: livestock, horses, smith
tools, wagon, household kitchen items, household
furniture, 1000# bacon, negros, leather, iron-bound
trunk, 2000# tobacco, one book "Revis Code of Laws",
one Bible, one slate, cotton, needles, buttons, pins,
shoe buckles, 2 sets of pistols, money scales, one
rifle gun. A parcel of tools in the possession of
Francis Spalden. Debts due on open account:
Robert Pennington, Elizabeth Salsburg, Martin Amis' Deck,
Peter Hale, Joel Bundren, Joseph Hurt, Isaac Hollandsworth,
John Medley, Claburn Nash, Thomas Mitchell, Samuel Amos,
Philip Stevens, James Thomas Jr, John Perdey, deceased,
Thomas Oldham, Nathaniel Morison, William Ross, John Deal,
John Danniel, William Parsons, John Mankins, Nathan Harris,
William Solsbury, David P. Brannam, Stephen Maner, Mathew
Morrow, Pilson's Tobe, Moses Godard, William James Mayo,
Andrew Breden, David Parmer, Zeph Goin, Richard Davis,
Abrah. Meele, Joseph Meredey, James Harris, Thomas Spencer,
Jacob Blackburn, John Bellemey, David Eusley, John Hanby,
Jr., Abel Mede Jr, Jesse Mede, Capt Foster's George,
William Ryan, Hickman Edwards, John Whaling, Jeremiah
Stone, Richard Deal, Sarah Via, James Taylor Jr., Isham
Edward, Edward Helton, Robert Frasher, Richard Whaling,
James Pelphrey, Thomas Hill, David Howell, Joseph Mapes,
John Fenney, John Corn son of George, Izbel Airs(Ayres),
Bennet Houchins, Capt. William Adams, Thomas Craddock,
Cornelius Thomas, Richard Vaun, Gabriel Dehart, William
Price deceased, James Whaling, Francis Thomson, Mary
Brammer, Benjamin Philpott, John Carter's Henry, William
Hale, Barnard M. Price, Jacob Blackburn, Samuel Medley,
William Pilson, William Wit, Sr., Abel Hancock, John
Whaling, Richard Sharp, William Sharp, David Taylor,
James Ingrum Jr. Moses Godard, Elias Bryant, Crawford
Burnet, Mildred Pennington, Ruben Short, Lewis Foster,
John Foster, Charles Foster Jr, Charles Foster Sr, John
Reavs, Josiah Reavs, Thomas Reavs, William Corn, William
Hancock, James Hollandsworth, John Cogs, Abel Peregoy,
Rhody Whaley, Alvern Luis, Isaac Martin, Edward Parmer,
Richard Barnard, John Adams Jr, Francis Heneley, Benjamin
Mayo, Malichi Commins, Zekel Perdy, Benjamin Mize,
Bennet Houchens, Daniel Macingtire and wife, David Ross,
James Taylor Jr, William Banks Sr, Thomas Sneed,
Richard Reynolds, Peter Finney, Thomas Hale, Marvel
Boling, John Glasbey, John Barrot, George Pigg, William
Banks Jr, Harvey Fitzgerald, Robert Boyd, Charles Rakes,
James Boling Jr, Obediah Stover, John Gilbert, Isaac
McBride, Isham Harris, Adam Turner, James Brammer,

Nathaniel Craddock, George Frasher, Thomas Spalden, John Tugle, Mallichi Parmer, Barnard M. Price, Isaac Mis(Mize) Enoch Bredwell, William Belile(Baslile), Oen (Owen) Griffe, Jurden Clay, Abner Hodge, William Thomson, Jiles Martin, James Coldman, William Coldman, Richard. Masse, James Deel, Christopher Foley, Richard Tommas, James Boling Jr, Sims' Phillip, Sims' Jeremiah, Burnet's Dick, Mrs. Lockhart's Tobe, Mrs. Lockart's Jude, Bartlett's Sam, Hall's Daniel, Burnet's Ben, Cornelius Burnet, Ruben Burnett, Samuel Hilton, Jeremiah Moles Jr, John Finney, Townley Rig, Paul C. Ingrum, Zalphiniah Tennison, William Walden, Benjamin Hickman, Barnard Belile, Joseph Meredy, Jacob Stover, Elisha Rakes, Reaha Pen, Capt Gabriel Pen, John Sharp Sr, John Adams, Jr, John A. Corn, William McCutchen, William Fuson Jr, Benjamin Hubbard, Thomas Tennison, Samuel Crutcher Sr, Robert Rite(Wright), Henry Dillion, Bassel's Nicholas.

Debts by Notes:
Ruben Short, Henry Farmer, Isaac Dotson, James McCutchen, Charles Hill, William Thompson, Thomas Boland, Joseph Reynolds, Bartlett Johns, Brett Stovall, George Martin, Green Penn, Thomas Penn, John Owen, William Willis, Joel Chitwood, Malicha Parmer, William Salsbury, Richard Sharp, Jeremiah Burnett, John Corn son of George, Francis Spalden, Joseph Moles, Barnard More Price, Nathaniel Ross, James Elkins & wife, John Termon, John Moles, James Commains, John Cherey, Philip Anglin, Samuel Martin, William Salsbury, William Frasher, John Hooker, John Bingman, Soloman Stevins, Bartlet Reynolds, John Spalden, William Stone, Joseph Breden, Joel Chitwood, James Cummings, Jeremiah Moles, James Boling, Thomas Hill, Joseph Miller, Thomas Smothers, Edward Luis, John Sharp, John Mankins, William Banks, Isaac Breden, Thomas Willis, John A. Corn, James Moles, David Taylor, Obediah Ascue, Benjamin Ramsey, Samuel Harris, Richard Nowlin, John James, Robert Lockhart, John Moles, John Chitwood, John Breden.

Signed: Charles Foster, William Fuson, John Hall, John Burnet, Thomas Reeves.
No total

Pg 263   Date: 11 May 1809
A further inventory of the estate of Jesse Corn, deceased Cattle and bonds on Colemen Ledbetter, William Harris, James Bird, Solomon Keaton, Zachariah Hale of Chesterfield County.
No total.

Pg 264   Date: 26 July 1810
Appraised estate of John Gates, deceased by Richard
Harrison, Samuel Crutcher, Thomas Penn.
Horses, cattle, kitchen items, household furniture,
parcel of old books, farming tools and equipment.
Total: L55.2.0
Returned: July Ct 1810

Pgs 265-266   Date: 5 Dec 1812
Inventory of the estate of James Murphy, deceased.
Household furniture, tools, kitchen and cooking
utensils, horse, cattle, saddle, farming equipment.
By M. Sandefur, Richard Harrison, Hamon Critz and
George Fulcher.
Total: $162.99
Returned: Dec Ct 1812

Pg 266   Date: 12 Feb 1814
Inventory of the estate of James Taylor by George
Fulcher, M. Sandefur, William Jones, John Clark.
Household items, bee stands, farming equipment,
furniture, cattle, saddle, horse.
Total: $116.68
Returned: Feb Ct 1814

Pg 267   Date: 5 May 1812
Inventory of the estate of John Cassaday, deceased by
John Tatum, Andrew Joyce, William Lee Sr, Joseph Newman.
Cart, cattle, horse, guns, tobacco 1300#, saddle,
kitchen items, flax wheel, cotton wheel, household
furniture.
Total: $ 228.24
Returned: ....Ct 1812

Pgs 268-269   Date: 29 March 1813
Inventory of William Perkins deceased by Adam Turner,
Charles Thomas Sr, Thomas R. Hall.
Includes: cattle, horses, wagon, smith tools, coopers
tools, turners tools, plantation tools, money scales,
one small trunk and some Doctors means, household
furniture, 2 shot guns, looking glass, slate, tract
of land whereon said Perkins lived last, one tract on
top of the mountain, tract in Montgomery Co. on the
head of Pine Creek, one house Bible, one Dixenary,
two other books, 21 pcs gold, 16 dollars in silver,
5 crowns, 7/3 in small money, 100 gallons Brandy,
Casks, bee stands.
Total: L468.16.6
Returned: April Ct 1813

Pg 270   Date: 21 Nov 1814
Inventory of the estate of Thomas Ayres, Sr.
Includes: household furniture, side saddle, kitchen items, bee gums, pack saddle, cotton wheel, tomahock, corn, sheep, cattle, horse, loom, books, hog.
Signed: William Carter, William Moore, James Dickerson, Thomas Whitlock, Jacob Griggs Administrator.
Total $ 185.80
Returned: Dec Ct 1814

Pg 271   Date: 6 Dec 1814
An inventory of property of Barbary Ayres, widow of Thomas Ayres, deceased, after a division.
Sheep, fodder, cooking utensils, household furniture, flax and cotton wheels, cow, tomhawk.
By Jacob Griggs, guardian
Total $56.64
Returned: Dec Ct 1814

Pgs 272-273   Date: 1 Feb 1814
Inventory estate of John Ingrum, deceased by John Hall, William Walden, Zaphaniah Tennison.
Includes: three negros, cattle, horses, sheep, saddles, house furniture, 1 linning wheel, 2 cotton wheels, shot gun, pouch and horn, cooking utensils, trunk, spice morter pessel, wheat sieve, Bible, humn book, sermon book, cotton cards, plows, tools, sheep shears.
No total
Returned: Feb Ct 1814

Pg 273   Date: 13 May 1814
Inventory estate of Robert Mayo deceased by James Fulkerson, John Rea, William Gray.
Includes: bay mare, feather bed and furniture, cotton wheel, cooking utensils, one saddle, shoe tools, 2 books, plantation tools.
Total: $73.15
Returned: May Ct 1814

Pg 274   Date: 12 Feb 1814
The estate of Obediah Harris deceased by Andrew Joyce, Nathaniel Smith, Barnard Harris, Robert Rogers.
1 gray mare $25.00
1# indigo   1.50   Total $26.50
Returned: May Ct 1814

Pg 274   Date: 4 Dec 1813
An inventory of the property of John Brammer, deceased.
one feather bed and furniture, 1 wool hat, 1 big coat,
1 knife and chisel, 1 clos body coat, one tract of
land. Total: $81.96
By Thomas R. Hall, Charles Thomas Sr, Hugh Boyd
Returned: Jan Ct 1814

Pg 275   Date: not listed
Inventory of the estate of Joseph Newman by John
Tatum, Nathaniel Smith, H. Fitzgerald.
Waggon, horses, plantation tools, cooking items,
house furniture, saddle, cotton wheel, flax wheel,
loom, cattle, sheep.
Total $243.71
Returned: May Ct 1815

Pg 276   Date: 22 July 1815
An inventory of the estate of Bennett Houchins, deceased
by Jeremiah Burnett, Isaac Adams, John Sneed.
Horse, sheep, steers, cattle, hogs, a still, house
furniture, cooking items, and one note on William
Burnett. Total $349.09
Returned: Aug Ct 1815

Pg 277   Date: 24 Oct 1815
Inventory of the estate of David Robertson, deceased by
Reuben Harris, Adam Turner, John Sneed
28 hd hogs, 2 mares, 2 cows and calves, 6 hd sheep,
2 negros, 1 rifle gun and shot pouch, 1 mans saddle,
case of bottles, 4 boxes, set of shoe makers tools,
1 hand saw, dressing knife, broad axe, auger & chisels,
3 beds and furniture, 3 sides of leather, 1 flax wheel
and cut reel, 2 chests, 1 honey stand, 2 flat irons and
bellows, 5 books, 1 pr money scales, 1 trunk, 2 candle
sticks, 2 locks, hammer, 1 cubboard, 2 bowls, cup and
saucers, coffee pot, pitcher, 3 glasses, 4 plates, 2
bottles, 5 vials, one cruet, 2 jugs, 1 butter pot,
pewter, 1 set knives & forks, 14 chairs and table, 2
skillets, 1 pr steelyeards, 1 steel trap, funnel, iron
tools, 2 axes, curry comb, 4 iron wedges, mattock,
bell, hoe, pr chains, 3 ploughs, 1 scythe & craddle,
potware, water vessels & bason, 1 beef hide, 1 set
blacksmith tools, cooper & carpenters & gun socking
tools, 7 head cattle.
Total $1,065.13
Returned: Nov Ct 1815

Pg 278   Date: 7 April 1815
An inventory of the estate of Nathan Hall, deceased by
Adam Turner, Richard Thomas, Charles Thomas Jr.
Includes: 10 negros, 2 horses, cows, furniture, 2 shot
guns, cooking utensils, 1 book of geography, 4 vollums
of Josephus, 2 dictionary, 5 other books, saddle,
linning wheel, cash in 3 dobbloons, 5 half io...,
6 gueneys inglish, 3 one dore, 3 french guneys, 3
quarter eagles, 1 half gueney and other small pieces.
No total
Returned: April Ct 1815

Pg 279   Date: 12 Dec 1815
Inventory of the estate of John Sneed deceased by
John Brammer, John Clarke, Thomas Tennison.
Beds and furniture, pewter, earthen ware, kitchen
cooking utensils, tools, cotton wheel, a bond on
William Sneed and one on John Spading.
Total: $341.11
Returned: Dec Ct 1815

Pg 280   Date:
Inventory of Munford Smith a convict in the penitentiary
house and public jail by Gabriel Penn, John Tatum,
P. Cardwell.
Includes: 4 beds and furniture, pewter, looking glass,
rifle gun, horses, hogs, wagon, smith tools, 6 negros,
6 negro children, an ox cart, cattle, sheep.
Total $3,399.33
Returned: March Ct 1816

Pgs 281-282   Date: 22 Dec 1815
Inventory of the estate of William Smith by William
Carter, Samuel Hanby, Harvey Fitzgerald.
Includes: hogs, cattle, oxen, sheep, wheat, 2500# tobacco,
plantation tools, house furniture, books, 2 negros, 8
negro children, silver watch, double barrel gun, 2 shot
guns, one 70 gallon still, cash in Tatum's hands,
saddle, cash in hands of Munford Smith, one bond on
Nathaniel Smith. John Smith Administrator.
No total
Returned: Jan Ct 1816

Pg 283   Date: 19 Apr 1816
Inventory estate of Joshua Haynes, deceased by Abr. Penn,
Jesse Mankin, Phillip Anglin.
Hogs, horses, cattle, rifle gun, saddle, household items.
Returned: May Ct 1816

Pgs 284-285   Date: 13 Aug 1817
Inventory the estate of Jonathan Hanby, deceased by
John Tatum, Samuel Hanby, William Booker, Jacob Hudson.
Includes: desk bookcase, two tables, cupboard, 10 chairs,
candle stand, cooking utensils, books, 1 case razor and
hone, five beds and furniture, bee stands, plantation
tools, five negros, blacksmith tools, 1 yoak of steers,
cattle, hogs, sheep, geese.
Total: $2,267.42
Returned: Sept Ct 1817

Pg 285 - duplicate of pg 280 - Munford Smith

Pgs 286-287   Date: 3 Jan 1817
Inventory estate of James Nowlin by David Taylor,
Richard Harrison, Hamon Critz.
one negro, horses, cattle, hogs, tobacco, bee stands,
saddle and saddle bags, house furniture, looking glass,
kitchen utensils.
Total $813.00
Returned: Jan Ct 1817

Pg 287   Date: not listed
List of William Smith, Sr. property not inventoried by
the Commissioners.
Hogs, iron, geese, a bell and raw hide
No total
Returned: July Ct 1817

Pg 287   Date: not listed
List of William Smith Jr, not inventoried by the
Commissioners.
Corn, leather, skins, one fiddle, steel trap, shucks.
No Total - John Smith, Administrator
Returned: July Ct 1817

Pgs 288-289   Date: 16 Nov 1816
Inventory of James Ingrum, Senr., deceased
Hogs, cattle, sheep, horses, plantation tools, bee stands,
kitchen utensils, loom, 2 flax wheals, 2 cotton wheals,
16 chairs, 2 tables, 9 beds and furniture, large Bible,
7 small books, account on William Viar, account on
Alexander Ingrum, account on John Bell, 2 womans saddles,
account on Robert Akers, $2.00 received of Jeremiah Burnett,
1 firkin of butter, 1 parcel of dry meat, corn, wheat,
oats, 1 gun, saddle, horse, account of James Ingrum, Jr,
10 negros.
Martha Ingrum and Alexander Ingrum executors.

By Zephaniah Tennison, Edward Lewis, W. Massey
Total $4,296.03
Returned: Jan Ct 1817

Pg 290   Date: 11 Dec 1816
Inventory the estate of Noah Harbour by....
Corner cupboard, house furniture, cattle, tools, mare,
woman's saddle, kitchen utensils, two looking glasses,
bedding, quilts, counterpains, 3 books, furniture,
debts due the estate by account of John Turner, Samuel
Harris Sr, Thomas Harbour.
No total
Returned: Jan Ct 1817

Pg 291   Date: 24 June 1818
Inventory the estate of William Harris, Jr, deceased
by Thomas Reynolds, William Atkinson, M. Sandefur.
Cattle, hogs, furniture, Bible, plantation tools, loom,
spinning wheel, flax wheel, kitchen utensils.
Total $142.50
Returned: July Ct 1818

Pgs 292-293   Date: 24 Jan 1818
Inventory estate of George Fulcher deceased by M.Sandefur,
William Atkinson, John Clark, Thomas Reynolds.
Horses, hogs, cattle, sheep, plantation tools, house
furniture, kitchen utensils, books, shoe makers tools,
1 case razor, loom, flax wheel, cotton wheel, man and
womans saddle.
Total $292.87
Returned: Feb Ct 1818

Pg 293   Date: 24 Dec 1817
Inventory of Barbary Abshear, deceased, property sold by
me Jacob Griggs Administrator.
Kitchen utensils, cotton wheel, house furniture, cattle,
sheep.   Total $98.35
Returned: Jan Ct 1818

Pg 294   Date: 16 Jan 1819
Inventory John Johnston deceased by Thomas Whitlock,
Samuel Hanby, Jacob Grigg, Jesse Mankin.
Corn, house furniture, saddle, kitchen utensils, cattle,
pigs, sheep, horses.
Total $365.17
Returned: May Ct 1819

Pg 295   Date: 29 May 1818
Inventory of the estate of Elisha Cooper, deceased by
Samuel Packwood, Elisha Packwood, John Akers.
Horses, swine, loom, house furniture, two spinning wheels,
cattle, sheep, plantation tools.
Total $275.34
Returned: June Ct 1818

Pgs 296-298   Date: 22 Jan 1819
Inventory of the estate of Gabriel Penn, deceased by
M. Sandefur, J. Tatum, Thomas Cardwell
Steers, carts, cattle, sheep, hogs, 10 horses, leather,
plantation tools, kitchen utensils, 1 still, bee stands,
2 desks, bookcase, 1 clock, 1 silver watch, rifle gun,
shot bag, 7 feather beds and furniture, sundry books,
3 side saddles, 1 boys saddle, 1 mans saddle, corn,
wheat, rough food, pork, tobacco, 47 negros.
Total: $24,360.04
Returned: May Ct 1819

Pg 299   Date: 3 June 1819
Inventory of the estate of James Carter, deceased by
J. Tatum, George Laman, H. Fitzgerald, Samuel Howell.
2 negros, cattle, horse, bee stands, furniture.
No total
Returned: June Ct 1819

Pg 300   Date:
Inventory of John Johnson, deceased   by Charles Lewis
Sr and Jane Johnson administrators.
Horse, corn, cow and calf, house furniture, saddle, sows,
pigs, kitchen utensils.
Total $430.78
Returned: March Ct 1819

Pg 301   Date: 20 Feb 1819
Inventory of the estate of Clement Vaughter by William
Carter, Samuel Hanby, J. Tatum, James Howell.
Hogs, cattle, horse, 1 still, house furniture, coppers
tools, plantation tools, 8 books, 5 beds and furniture,
1 mans saddle, 1 womans saddle.
No total
Returned: May Ct 1819

Pg 302   Date:
Inventory the estate of William Jones deceased by Richard
Harrison, William Frans, Thomas Reynolds.
Hogs, horses, plantation tools, 3 saddles, yoke of steers,
cart, sheep, geese, ducks, 8 negros, rye, oats, corn, beef,
bacon, kitchen utensils, shotgun, 16 chairs, 6 beds and
furniture, leather and shoe makers tools.
Total $4,641.08
Returned: June Ct 1819

Pgs 303-304   Date: 16 Nov 1819
Inventory of the estate of Ignatious Sims deceased by
Jerman Baker, Edward Philpott, Euisbusous Stone.
27 negros, horses, oxen, cattle, hogs, sheep, 40 gallon
copper still, ox cart, mill saw, 1 rifle gun, 2 old
shot guns, kitchen furnishings, 5 beds and furniture,
18 setting chairs, 3 cotton wheels, 2 flax wheels,
4 saddles, 2 pr specttecls and case.
Total $11,338.--
Returned: Feb Ct 1820

Pg 305   Date: 15 April 1820
Inventory of the estate of free Harry Howard, a man of
colour.
Pots, dishes, knives, forks, cotton wheel and bedding.
Total $6.20
By John France, William France, Francis Harrison
Returned: June Ct 1820

Pgs 306-307   Date: 20 Dec 1819
Inventory of the estate of Benjamin Terry, deceased by
M. Sandefur, Isaac Adams, Samuel McAlexander and
Obediah Burnett administrator.
one cow, haff to Viney, 1 cow haff to Nancy, Bible,
house furniture, loom, 3 old books, testament, farming
equipment, 1 work steer called Buck, cattle, sheep,
pigs.
Total $219.35
Returned: Jan Ct 1820

Pg 308   Date: 13 Feb 1820
Inventory of the estate of John Adams, deceased by
Samuel Corn, John Slaughter, Isaac Martin.
Includes: 3 negros, cattle, horses, hogs, 1 still, loom,
tobacco, plantation tools, carpenters tools, bee hives,
cupboard furniture, books, house furniture, saddle and

saddle bags, sheep, geese, ducks, brandy, blacksmith
tools, beds and furniture, debts owing the estate.
Mary Adams and Joshua Adams executors.
Total $1,401.26
Returned: Feb Ct 1820

Pgs 309-310   Date: 5 Aug 1820
Inventory of the estate of Richardson Harrison, deceased
by Joseph Kennerly, Hamon Critz, John Frans.
6 negros, horses, hogs, house furniture, shot gun, 17
old books, looking glass, saddles, bed and furniture,
1 old still, steel rat trap, kitchen utensils, bacon,
cattle, sheep, Col. Richard Harrison for 3 cows and
1 steer, Jesse Murphy note due 25th Dec next, George
Harrison note, Francis B. Harrison note, account against
Col. G. Penn, the amount of which is in dispute.
No total
Returned: Nov Ct 1820

Pg 311   Date: 4 Dec 1820
Inventory of property of Thomas Dillard deceased by
Munford Smith, Joseph Smith, Thomas Whitlock.
Corn, hogs, smith tools, flax, horses, sheep, bee stands,
plantation tools, flax, horses, rifle gun, 1 shot gun,
3 negros, house furniture, saddle bags, spinning wheels,
leather, wool and cloth, wheat, oats, rye, cattle, guinia
fowl, a parcel of planks at Moor's saw mill.
No total
Returned: Sept Ct 1821

Pgs 313-314   Date: 25 Dec 1820
Inventory of the estate of Jerman Baker deceased by
Joseph Kennerly, Gregory Hagood, Edward Philpott
59 bags of manufactured tobacco, 1 gig and harness,
leaf tobacco, hogs, steers, cattle, plantation tools,
dressing glass, looking glass, 1 silver chain and seal,
6 Winsor chairs, 2 chears, shot gun, bed and furniture,
corner cupboard, horses, 1 still, 7 negros, two $50.00
Virginia notes, 50¢ bill of North Carolina, one note
of $6.61 on Thomas Hollandsworth, bond on John Shelton,
William F. Abington for $500.00, bond on Daniel Harris,
John D. Marshall, note on Edward M. Booker, check on
L. M. Taliferro at Rocky Mount, note on John Cannaday,
wagon harness, fiddle, new wagon, gun barrel and gun
lock.
No total
Returned: June Ct 1821

Pgs 315-316   Date: 21 Sept 1820
Inventory of the estate of John Tuggle Sr, deceased by
M. Sandefur, Jeremiah Burnett, James Via, Adam Turner.
Saddle bags, kitchen utensils, beds and furniture,
household furniture, shot gun, dry fruit, old still,
flax wheel, wheat, rye, benas, cotton wheel, bear trap,
plantation tools, salt, horses, cart, yoke of oxen,
cattle, smith tools, five negros, steel traps, hogs,
working steer, flax, corn, sheep and hemp.
No total
Returned: Feb Ct 1821

Pgs 317-319   Date: 23 Aug 1821
Inventory of the estate of Peter Scales, deceased by
P.D. Scales, Nathaniel Scales Administrators.
Sheep, ten horses, 1 road waggon, 1 little wagon, ox
cart, ox cart and 2 yokes, window glass, mill spindle,
steel trap, 80 bushels salt, bear skin, 29 old flour
barrels, womans saddle, mans saddle, rocking cradle,
1 silver watch, 8-day clock, tea table, 17 chairs,
silver table, tea and soup soups, wooden vessels in
dairy, waffle irons, 9 old books, 2 maps, beds and
furniture, saddle bags, seals and weights, money scales,
bacon, 1 mill wrights guide, work steers, cattle, hogs
wheat, 16 negros.
No total

Pgs 320-322   Date:
An inventory of part of the estate of Peter Scales,
Bonds on the following due from 1786-1820
Joseph Martin, Joseph Scales, Tap. Nelson, John Ridley,
Samuel Doyle, Robert Chandler, Walter Brooks, Allen Thomas,
Richard Thomas, Robert Law, John Redman, John Reed, John
Woods since deceased, Arza. Hutchisin, William Walker,
Thomas Johnson, John Ridley, Erasmus Alley Jr, Alexander
Joyce, George Tucker, Jesse Couch, John Campbell, Bosha
Harvey, Benjamin Shival ?, Daniel Witt, George Gibson,
John Davice. An order from Elizabeth Taylor to Greens-
ville Penn, an order from Pleasants Scales to Peter
Scales. Mary Hughes book account, John King runaway,
Thosp. Lacy, John Matlocks runaway, William Heath's
runaway, The following names all have runaway following
them: John Switzer, William Harris, Lavinia Brewer,
John Bellamay, Henry Baker Jr, Gideon Gilley, William
Brooks, Benjamin Hawkins, Henry Phillips, Nathaniel
Elgar, Thomas Doss, Robert King, W. V. Snyder.
The following lists apparently had accounts with Mr. Scales.
Gabriel Penn, William Atkinson, Samuel Martin, William
Morris, Reuben Hughes, George S. Staples, Eramus Alley,

Joseph Martin of Henry, John Fodril Harden Hairston, James Mrans, John Redley, Thomas Smith, Obed. Harris, Bardel Alley, Jesse Simmons, John Rea, Andrew Frye, Jeremiah Cloud, John Staples, Robert Chandler, William Matthews, Robert Law, John Walker insolvent, William Gates, German Baker, Mary Vernen, John Campbell, John Simmons, Rice Brown, Peter Hairston, John Joyce Jr son of Possum, Michael Burres, Edward Lan, Alexander Dodson, John N. McMillon, John Hughes, James Penn, Greensville Penn, John Kallam, Alice Brown, Henry Koger, Jeremiah Hutcherson, James Bohannon, Edward C. Staples, Satney Amos, Josiah Leak, Milly Cox, John Shaffer, Madison R. Hughes, William Jennings, Daniel Hutchinson, Robin Tucker, John Koger, Leander Hughes, Hezekiah Farr, Peter F. Leak, Henry Fee, James Martin Jr, John Kington, Daniel Witt, Johnson Going, Samuel Dalton, Christopher Standly, Daniel Fagg, John Ragan, Lydia Joyce, Washington Amos, Reuben Moore, Thomas Going, William Steel, Charles Foster, Hyder A. Rogers, Joel Cardwell, John Phillips, Thomas J. Wooten, Wilson S. Vernon, Nathaniel Scales, Richard Webster, William Mills son of Richard, John Scales, David Taylor, Richard C. Alley, John Powers, Michael Reed, David Kallam Sr, David Kallam Jr, Benjamin Hinnes, Nathan Going.
Money deposited by Z. King
Judgement against David Rea
Judgement against Elijah Trent
Returned: Nov Ct 1821

Pg 323   Date: 25 May 1822
Inventory of the estate of Augustine Thomas deceased by Powell Gray, John Rea, Richard Mills.
Hogs, 8 horses, flax 90 barrels of corn, wheat, tobacco, plantation tools, cattle, blacksmith tools, household furniture, shot gun, rifle and shot bag, hides, clock, large corner cupboard, 2 looking glasses, parcel of books, saddle bags, house furniture, kitchen utensils, a still, 1 little wagon, 1 big wagon, salt, cotton, leather, vinegar, looms and wheels, 12 negros, bacon, sheep, 236 dollards and 4 half joes in hand, one bond $30.80.
Returned: Oct Ct 1822

Pgs 326-327   Date: 10 June 1822
Inventory estate of William McAlexander, Sr., deceased by M. Sandefur, W. Ayres, John Massey, Gabriel Boling.
6 negros, cattle, yoke of oxen, cart, hogs, horses, blacksmith tools, still, sheep, geese, plantation tools, hemp and flax, kitchen utensils, 14 chairs, 12 pewter

basins, wooden clock, looking glass, books, flax, wool
and cotton, 4 old saddles, furniture, 12 woolen couter-
panes, 1 feather bed and furniture to Milly, 23 yards
home made cloth, 16 yards tow cloth, 1 old ship saw.
Jesse Jones, executor.   Total $2,043.37
Returned: Aug Ct 1822

Pg 328   Date: 28 June 1819
Inventory the estate of William Moore, deceased.
Horses, cows, 1 china priss and desk, tables, desk,
6 w. chairs, clock, 1 gilt looking glass, dressing
glass, 12 split bottom chairs, 7 beds and furniture,
waffle iron, common shot gun, 1 fowling piece, large
cherry table, plantation wagon, other wagon, road
wagon, 1 old Gigg, blacksmith tools, 150# cotton,
1 small kegg of paint Spanish Brown, 32 gal barrel
wiskey, 70# butter, family Bible, cambrick, calico,
nankee, bumbast, dimity, flannel, cotton casemere,
shackemett, swansdown, silk, ribbon, knives, gunlocks,
watch, gimblet, desk mountain. B. buckles, pewter
buckles, thimbles, shoes, locks, razor cases, pen knives,
buttons, file, pins, glasses, allum, bridle bits, snuff
boxes, shoe tacks, combs, tea spoons, brushes, soap,
scales, tin pans, funnels, buckets, coffee pots, shoes,
trumpet, hat, disher, plates, dishes, cup and saucers,
tumblers, salt sellars, pen knives, drachin glasses,
ointment, borax, b. oil spanish brown, pistols, lead,
logwood, teaboard, cards, chest.
The alterations made at the instance of Capt. W. Carter.
Made by J. Tatum, A. Staples, Jacob Grigg.
William Carter J. Administrator
Returned: Nov Ct 1821

Pg 329   Date: 19 Nov 1821
Additional appraisment of the estate of Peter Scales
by John Rea, Richard Mills, Samuel Hughes.
Fodder, oats, flax, tobacco, blacksmith tools, fire
dogs, 145 barrels corn.
Returned: Feb Ct 1822

Pg 330   Date: 30 Sept 1819
Inventory of William Moore in Patrick and Grayson Counties
by Thomas Whitlock, Jacob Grigg, Joseph Smith.
Plantation tools, 100 head of hogs, 21 hd of cattle, 2
cribs corn, 250 bu rye, oats, house full of shucks,
12 horses, 1 waggon, 1 pistol, kitchen utensils, smith
tools, mill saw, houseful of tobacco, tomahawk, house
furniture, wheat 100 gal. cider, 30 yds homespun,

saddle bags, cattle, 70 head hogs, 65 head sheep,
1 still, 1 new wagon, 1 3-horse wagon, 675# iron,
bearskin, shoe leather, old still, large still,
waggon, yoke of oxen, oats, cattle, rocking cradle.
William Carter, administrator
Returned: Nov Ct 1821

Pg 333   Date:
Sales of property of William Moore, deceased in Patrick
County 26 June 1819, four sales. Sales to:
Gilbert Bowman, Samuel Flippen, Drury Hanks, Henry Bays,
William Carter, James McCraw, Nehemiah Prater, Reuben
Branscomb, Martin Cloud, William Cloud, Vernon Sampson,
Elijah Dickinson, James Smith, H. H. Moore, Mitchell
Ahart, John Thompson, Drury East, Samuel Moore, Sarah
Hanby, John Hix, Thomas Snow, Leonard Owen, James Boyd,
Hiram Bolt, Thomas Ayres, William McCraw, James Puckett,
Hail Snow, S. R. Webb, Henry Deen, Martin Bolt, James
Brim, John Eaton, Micajah Forkner, Samuel Walker, Joseph
Boyd, William McMillion, Dabney Walker, Bartlett Smith,
J. V. Griggs, Jonston Snow, Claborn Harris, James
Smith, Thomas Snow, Isham Puckett, Fielding Bayson,
John Webb, William Sutfin, William Reynolds, James Martin,
Bart. Smith, Joseph Gowen, Caleb Carron, Stephen McKinney,
James Lyon, William Carter Jr, Galeheu Moore, Hale Snow,
William McCraw (Buck), Moses Grigg, Dudley McMillin,
Isham Barnard, William Bays Jr, Bengen Reynolds, John
Robertson, David Love, Evon Jones, William Edwards,
James Brown, Jacob Horton, Jonathan Herald, John Bolt Jr,
Aaron Bowman, James Deerman, Sarah Hanby, John Eperson,
William Carter Sr.,
Rent of home place to H. H. Moore
Rent of Christian place to H. H. Moore
Rent of Johnston Crk. place to Thomas Ayres
Rent of Robertson place to John Bolt
4th sale to: Edmond Beasely, William Hanby, Jacob Ahart,
John Hix, Joseph Smith, Benjamin R. Landrith, Elisha
Edwards, James Norton, Isaac Pike, William Clark,
John Cole, Elk. Ayres, Munford Smith, John Bowman.
Grayson County: Jonathan Jennings, Samuel Brown,
Jona. Richardson Sr., James Jones, William Williams,
William Gorden, John Hill, Robert Jennings, Jesse
Borwn, Caleb Babet, James Shockley, Adam Hall.

Pgs 343-344
William Moore sale - cont'd
William Grigg, Elijah Edwards, James Dillard, George
Cloud, Maj. Carter, Nathaniel Bryson, Maj. Forkner,
John Martin, James Bolt, Thomas Whitlock, Anderson
J. Grigg, Joseph V. Grigg, Jacob A. McCraw, James W.
McCraw.

Items sold include: cattle, horses, cloth, buttons, watch, buckles, shoes, scissors, shaving glass, teaspoons, shaving soap, money scales, coffee pots, gun flints, prucian blue, british oil, spanish bottled oil, pistols, lead, tea, waggons, corn, gigg, cherry press, winsor chairs, hogs, rye, smith tools tables, furniture.
Rent of Hunts place to John Dalton
Rent of place where Drury East lived that was called McCraws place to Drury East.
Returned: Nov Ct 1821

Pg 344   Date:
Inventory of T. J. Penn and Greensville Penn, infants and heirs of Gabriel Penn, deceased for whom Thomas Penn is guardian. Negros in his charge are: Bob, Jennett and child, Henry, Harrison, Nelly, Tom, George, Kitty, Caroline, Wiatt, Jim and Jerman.
Returned: March Ct 1823

Pg 345   Date: 30 Jan 1823
Inventory of the estate of Clement Rogers, deceased by Jacob Hudson, William Booker, John Jones.
Includes pigs, cattle, steers, corn, flax, plantation tools, flax wheel, loom, bed and furniture, rifle gun and powder horn, household furniture.
Returned: Feb Ct 1823

Pgs 346-347   Date: 20 Feb 1823
Inventory of the estate of James Bartlett, deceased by Richard Thomas, Jesse Corn, John Hall, William Cannaday.
Includes, 2 horses, ox cart and yoke of steers, still, rye, wheat, flax, hemp, corn, pigs, cattle, bee stands, house furniture, saddle bags, 2 pr spectacles, razors, looking glass, kitchen utensils, books, Bible, one bond on Edmund Bartlett; one bond on George Washington; one bond on Cheley Rakes; a tittle bond on Edmund Bartlett for 100 acres of land in Kentucky on Willins Creek, paid in advance $162.74, balance $63.00.
Returned: May Ct 1823.

Pg 348   Date: 28 Oct 1823

Inventory of the estate of Hannah Smith, deceased.
Includes:
Hogs, cattle, corn, leather, sheep shears, saws, tools, sweet potatoes, yarn, pepper box, tobacco, peas, rye, horse and wheat.
By: Levi Clinkscales, Jacob Hudson, Samuel Martin, Munford Smith Administrator.
Returned: Dec Ct 1823

ABINGTON
  Taylor 34
  William F. 73

ABRAM-ABRAHAM
  Coss 18

ABSHEAR
  Barbary 70

ADAMS
  Elenor 22
  Elisha 21,41,42
  Elizabeth 25
  George 41
  H. 19
  Hannah 21, 42, 60
  Jacob 22,40,61,62
  *Jacob,Sr. 12,22
  James 37
  *John 22,25,37,41,62,72
  John,Jr. 37,41,63,64
  Joseph 21,41,42
  *Joshua 2,25,37,43,73
  *Isaac 6,21,23,40,41,43,
     57,67,72
  Leathy 21, 41, 42, 61
  Mary 22, 37, 73
  Nancy 21,31
  Paul C. 37
  Peggy 25
  Peter 22
  Polly 21, 41, 42
  Roland H. 37
  Sarah 23, 27
  Susannah 21
  Thomas 21, 41,42
  William, Capt., 63
  William 21,23,40,41,42,62
  William, Sr 21

AHART
  Adam 59
  Baines 59
  Jacob 77
  Mitchell 77

AKERS
  Hutson 60
  John 71
  Nancy 18
  Nathaniel 55
  *Stephen 18, 20

ALEB
  Joseph 1

ALEXANDER
  John 42

ALLEN
  Pines 60

ALLEY, ALLY
  Bardel 75
  Eleven 59
  Eramus 74
  Erasmus, Jr 74
  Richard C. 59,75

AMBOUR
  E.V. 59

AMOS
  Samuel 63
  Satney 75
  Washington 75

ANDERSON
  John 57

ANGLIN
  Adren 16
  *Adron 28
  Elisha 28
  Elizabeth 28
  Elizabeth, Sr 28
  Jane 28
  John 28, 31
  Lydia 28
  Naaman 28
  Phillip 28,51,58,64,68

ARNOLD
  Benjamin 1

*indicates Devisor

ASHLIN
  Cheslin 52
  Chesley 51

ASKEW
  Alexander 44
  John 44,46
  Obediah 64

ATKINSON
  Jesse 31
  Joseph 31
  Richard 8
  Stephen 51,56
  William 44,70,74

AYRES
  Barbary 66
  Capt. 58
  Elihu 58
  Elisha 44
  Elizabeth 30
  Elkanah 47,58,77
  Izbel 63
  John 62
  Lemuel 58
  Murphy 48
  Thomas 47,77
  Thomas Sr. 66
  W. 75
  William 35,55,57,58

BABET
  Caleb 77

BAILEY
  James 1
  Washington L. 60

BAKER
  *David 10,14,16
  James 14
  German 16,75
  Jerman 43,51,52,55,59,
    72,73
  Jeremiah 51,52,60
  Henry Jr. 74
  William 14,16

BALDSWIN
  Thomas 58

BALISLE
  Barnard 64
  William 62, 64

BALLARD
  Asa 56,59
  William, Jr. 58
  William Sr. 58

BANKS
  E. 61
  W. 21,41,61
  William 1,17,42,62,64
  William Jr. 40,63
  William Sr. 63

BANNISTER
  Joseph 15

BARDALE
  Enoch 59

BARNARD
  Isham 77
  Richard 63

BARRETT, BARROTT
  Francis 12
  Isham 59
  John 63

BARNET, BARRNET
  Sally 1

BARTLETT
  Ann C. 36,55
  Edmund 55,78
  James Jr. 36,55
  *James Sr. 35,55,78
  Moses 36
  Nancy G. 36,55
  Sally 36
  Temperance 35
  Thomas 36

BARTON
  Lydda 23
  Nancy 21,23
  Patsy 23
  Seppy 23
  Sharp 23
  Thomas 23
  William 12,23,24,41,61

*Devisor

BAULDEN
  E. 51

BAYLES
  William Jr. 58

BAYS
  Beverly 58
  Henry 77
  James 45
  William 58
  William Jr. 77

BAYSON
  Fielding 77

BEASLEY, BEAZLEY
  Edmond 77
  Hannah 19
  Richard 46
  Shadrack 19
  Thomas 19

BELCHER
  Obediah 48

BELL
  John 60,69
  Nathan 11

BELLAMAMY, BELLEMEY
  John 63,74

BELLER
  Eli 8,13,15
  *Elijah 8,15
  Elisha 27,45
  Nancy 15
  Peter 15,45,58,61
  Rachel 8

BENTON
  Sharp 12

BERNARD
  Archalous 37

BINGHAM
  John 58,64

BLACKBURN
  Jacob 63

BLANSETT
  William 53

BLOPANS?
  Bubby 35

BOAZ
  Elizabeth 37
  James Jr. 31
  James Sr. 31
  Robert 38,53

BOHANNON
  James 75
  John 44

BOLAND
  Thomas 64

BOLLING, BOWLIN, BOWLING
  Edmond 19
  Elizabeth 33
  Fanny 19
  Gabriel 35,47,57,75
  James 11,64
  James Jr. 63,64
  Marvel 47,55,63
  Rebecca G. 19
  Thomas 55,57,62

BOLT
  Charles 58,61
  Charles Jr. 45
  Hiram 59,77
  James 59,77
  John 50,52,77
  Martin 77

BONDURANT
  Drury 25

BOOKER
  Edward M. 73
  William 45,69,78

BOOTH, BOOTHE
  Bejah 35
  Mary 35
  Nancy 35
  Sarah 35

BOTETOURT
  John 1

BOWMAN
  Aaron 44,58,77
  Gilbert 44,45,46,77
  Hamon 58
  Hayman 45
  John 77
  John Jr. 58
  Leonard 59
  Norman 44
  Peter

BOYD
  Hugh 27,67
  James 77
  John 58
  Joseph 77
  Nancy 42
  Nanney 26
  Robert 63
  William 45

BRADLEY
  Rebecca 34

BRAMMER
  Burgess 27
  Edward 27
  Frances 33
  Frankey 27
  Hannah 35
  James 63
  John 68
  John Jr. 27
  *John Sr. 27,43,67
  Lucy 33
  Mary 63
  Shadrack 57
  William 56

BRANSCOMB
  James 58
  Reuben 58,77

BRANNAM
  David P. 63

BRANSON
  John 52

BREDEN
  Agnes 10
  Andrew 10,63
  Darcus 10
  Isaac 10,64
  James 10,15
  Jane 14
  Jean 10
  John 10,14,15,64
  *John Sr. 10,14,15
  Joseph 10,64
  Margret 10
  Mary 10
  Polly 35

BREDWELL
  Enoch 64

BREWER
  Lavinia 74

BREYDON
  Polly 35

BRIM
  James 77
  Joseph 44,59

BROOKS
  Walter 74
  William 74

BROWN
  Alice 75
  Betsey 38
  James 77
  Jesse 58,77
  *John 38
  Mary 38
  Nancy 34
  Noah 38
  Rice 75
  Samuel 77

BRYANT
  Elias 63
  Lydda 25
  Ruth 6

BUNDREN
  Joel 63

BUNDURANT
  Joel 44

BURCH
  John W. 59

BURGE
  William 14,19,46
  Woody 12

BURNETT
  Cornelius 64
  Crawford 47,63
  Jeremiah 36,55,64,67,69,74
  Jeremiah Jr. 30
  Jeremiah Sr. 1
  John 6,63,64
  Martha 23
  Nancy 33
  Micajah 6
  Obediah 47,48,72
  Reuben 64
  William 20,40,42,43,45,57,
    62,67

BURRESS, BURROUS
  Deborah 39
  John 51
  Michael 75

BYRD, BIRD
  *Abraham 2,5
  James

BRYSON
  Nathaniel 77

CAMPBELL
  John 74,75
  Sally 26

CAMRON
  Elizabeth 33
  Frankey 33
  *John 33
  Joseph 33
  Samuel 45

CANADAY, CANNADAY
  James 42,45
  John 73
  William 36,47,55,78

CANNON
  William 59

CARDWELL
  Joel 75
  John 46
  P. 68
  Perren 44
  Thomas 71

CARLAN
  James 8

CARR
  Benjamin 15

CARREL, CARROL
  Benjamin 46
  Elizabeth 35

CARRON
  Caleb 77

CARTER
  Capt. George 53
  Capt. W. 76
  Elizabeth 50
  George 12,48
  James 48,71
  Janey 33
  Jedediah 14
  *Harris 14,16
  John 52,60
  John P. 56
  Major 49,77
  William, Major 42,59
  Mary 59
  Nancy 14,16,33
  Silas 44,48
  Thomas 59
  William 1,6,8,11,12,13,16
    19,20,30,42,44,47,48,50,
    52,54,58,59,65,68,71,77
  William Jr 45,47,48,56,76
    77
  William Sr 44,45,48,58,77

CASSADAY
  John 65

CHAMBERS
  Agnes 27
  John 27

CHANDLER
　Robert 74,75

CHITWOOD
　Joel 21,64
　John 64

CHEREY
　John 64

CLABOURN, CLAIBORNE
　H. 51
　Nathaniel H. 8,52

CLARK, CLARKE
　George 62
　Jesse 43,62
　John 24,65,68,70
　Samuel 1,2,3,62
　William 24,48,58,77

CLAY
　Jurden 64

CLINKSCALES
　Levi 51,53,79

CLOUD
　George 77
　Jeremiah 75
　Martin 47,58,77
　William 77

COALSON
　Daniel 53

COCKRAM
　Nathan 42,45

COCKREL
　Frances 23

COGAR　see KOGER

COFFIN
　Barnabas 11

COGS
　John 63

COLEMAN, COLDMAN
　James 64
　William 64

COLE
　John 77

COLLIER, COLIER, COYLER
　Grizzle 22
　Jean 21

COLLINGS
　Anthony 13
　Daniel 46
　Edward 46
　Elijah 24,62
　John 24
　*Thomas 11,13,14
　William 11,13,46

COOK
　Isham 46
　Robert 56

COMMINS, COMMONS
　James 64
　Malichi 63
　Robert 22

CONNER
　John 15,43
　Lucy 38
　William 47

COOMER
　William 19

COOPER
　Elisha 71
　Mary 22

CORN
　Elizabeth 24,37
　George 1,62,63,64
　Jesse 14,15,55,64,63,78
　Jesse Jr 43
　Jesse Sr 18,40
　John 24,63,64
　John A. 40,43,64
　Milly 41
　Nancy 9
　Phebe 37
　Peter 1
　Samuel 24,44,62,72
　William 63

COUCH
　Jesse 74

COX
  James 23,31,42,45
  Mary 52
  Milly 75

CRADDOCK
  Isham 3,7,8
  James 43
  Nathaniel 64
  Thomas 63

CRAIG
  Robert 57

CRITZ, CRITZE
  Frederick 48,56
  Gabriel 51
  H. 57
  Hamon 1,2,8,18,26,34,38
    40,65,69,73
  Hamon Sr. 48
  Jacob 6,61
  Peter 59
  William 38,57

CROWIHER
  Elizabeth 30

CRUTCHER
  Elizabeth 26
  Samuel 65
  Samuel Sr 64

CRUMP
  Mary 24

CUMMINS, CUMMINGS
  James 64
  Joseph 6,7,10,16,60
  Moses 30
  Verlinda 22

CUSTER
  David 51

DALTON
  John 59,78
  Samuel 75

DANIEL
  John 63
  Nehemiah 22
  Robert 58

DAVIS, DAVICE
  Benjamin 60
  John 74
  Peter 60
  Rachel 47
  Richard 63
  Susannah 23
  William 60

DAVIDSON
  Golden 12
  Richard 13

DEAL
  James 40,64
  John 63
  Lucy 40
  Richard 63
  Sally 40
  William 40,41,62

DECK
  Martin Amis 63

DEEN
  Henry 77

DEERMAN
  James 77

DEHART
  E. 57
  Elijah 35,42,45,47
  Gabriel 63
  Jesse 35,47,55

DENNY
  Esther 1
  James 1,4

DESHAZO
  Henry 62

DETHERIDGE
  Acheles 54

DEWEESE, DEWEES
  Bartley 5
  *Cornelius 4,5,6
  Dawry 5
  Elizabeth 2
  Mary 5
  William 5

DICKERSON
  James 9,47,66
  Jean 9
  Mary 40

DICKINSON
  Elijah 77

DILLARD
  Edward 52
  James 45,52,77
  John 51
  Thomas 45,52,73

DILLION, DILLON
  Carrington 51,60
  Henry 64

DODSON, DOTSON
  Alexander 75
  George C. 48
  Isaac 64
  Lambert 51

DOSS
  Thomas 74

DOYLE
  Samuel 74

DRAPER
  Joseph 58
  William 60

DUVALL
  John 53

DYER
  David 60
  James 60

EADS
  Abraham 1

EASLEY
  *Ann, 8,9
  David 63
  John 8
  Joseph 8,9
  Warham 8,9,13
  William 13

EAST
  Drury 58,77,78
  William 58

EATON
  John 22,58,77

EDENS
  Agnes 15
  David 15
  Elexander 15
  Elizabeth 15
  Frances 15
  *John 15
  Ledy 15
  Mary 15
  John 15
  Nancy 15
  Sary 15
  Tabytha 15

EDWARDS
  Elijah 77
  Elisha 59,77
  Isham 63
  James 58
  William 58,77

ELGAR
  Nathaniel 74

ELGIN
  John 47

ELLIS
  Josiah S. 44,55

ELKINS
  James 64

ELLYSON
  *John 11,12,13,16
  Sally 11
  *Thomas 11,12,16

ELSICK
  Jonathan 44

ENGLISH
  John 44

ENNIS
  Early 58

EPPERSON
  James Jr. 21
  James Sr. 21
  John 45,46,77

EVENS
  Charles 15

FAGG
  Daniel 75

FAIN
  William 1

FARMER
  Henry 64

FARR
  Hezekiah 75

FARREL, FERRELL
  C.H. 39,56
  James 40,41
  John 1,2

FARRIS
  Josiah 8

FEE
  Henry 75

FENDLY
  Ceasar 33

FERGUSON
  Samuel H. 60

FERRIS
  Josiah 30,41,61

FIELDS
  James 44
  John 46

FINNEY
  Alexander 23
  John 8,10,63,64
  Peter 63

FITZGERALD
  H. 71
  Harvey 44,48,63,67,68
  Thomas 53

FLANIGAN
  John 15

FLEMING
  W. 57

FLETCHER
  John 4
  Miriam 24

FLIPPEN
  Samuel 45,50,58,59,77

FLOWERS
  Thomas 17

FODRELL
  John 75
  Samuel 53

FOLEY
  Baberry(Barbary 2
  Barbary Sr. 5
  *Bartholomew 2
  Bartlett 2,4
  Biddy 2
  Briget 5
  Christopher 64
  Mary 2
  Nelly 2
  Rachel 2

FORKNER
  Maj. 77
  Micajah 77

FOSTER
  Capt. George 63
  Charles 18,23,28,40,55,
    63,64,75
  Charles Jr. 40,55,59,63
  Charles Sr. 63
  Jancee 28
  John 63
  Lewis 40,60,63

FRANCIS, FRANCES
  John 30
  Polly 30
  Sucky 8

FRANKLIN
  Dr. B. 53
  John 60

FRANS, FRANSE
  Daniel 30,55
  Harriette 38
  Henry 3
  John 8,48,61,72,73
  John Jr 41
  *Mary 30
  Melkijah 46
  Peter 10
  Susannah 32,33,38
  William 33,72

FRASURE, FRAZER
  *Abraham 1,13,59
  Benjamin 59
  George 64
  Polly 13
  Robert 63
  Thomas 5,13
  William 64

FREEMAN
  Moses 8

FRY, FRYE
  Andrew 75
  John 45

FULCHER
  George 18,65,70

FULTON
  Rachel 30

FULKERSON
  *Frederick 3,6
  James 3,46,56,66
  Milly 3

FUSON
  James 25
  Sally 22
  Thomas 22
  William 6,25,33,62,63,64
  William Jr 64

GAINS
  Francis T. 46
  James S. 9,13,16,20
  Judith 8
  Pendleton 46
  Thurston 46

GARREN
  Peter 45

GARRETT see GEURRANT
  Joshua W. 49
  William 50

GARVAN, GARVIN
  Arthur 47,57

GATES
  John 65

GEARHART
  Valentine 36

GEURRANT
  Peter 42

GILBERT
  John 63
  Samuel 53

GIBSON
  James 51
  Jeremiah 15
  George 74

GILLEY
  Gideon 74

GILLIAM
  Jean 33
  Nancy E. 33
  Susannah 33

GILMER, GILMORE
  Peachey R. 52,58
  P.R. 27,44,46,48

GLASAPY
  John 40,63

GODARD
  Moses 63

GOIN, GOINS
  Arthur 25
  Betsy 25
  Isaac 25
  *James 25,61
  Nancy 25
  Prudence 25
  Stephen 25
  William 25
  William Sr. 59
  Zeph. 63

GOING, GOINGS
  Anthony 58
  Benjamin 58
  Caleb 19
  David Smith 19
  Fanny 19
  Claborn 19
  James 19
  Jerushe 19
  John 19
  Johnsohn 75
  Keziah 19
  Hannah 19
  *Nathan 2,5,12,13,51,75
  Obediah 19
  Rebeccah 19
  *Shadrack 2,12,19,20
  Soloman 19
  Thomas 59,75

GOLDING
  William 58

GORDON
  William 77

GOSSETT, GUSSETT
  Abraham 40
  John 10

GOWEN
  Joseph 77

GRAVELY
  Peyton 56

GRAY
  Daneil 40,59
  Elijah 53,59
  James 40
  John 26
  Joseph 33,44,46
  Mary 40
  Powell 41,75
  *William 6,40,59,66

GREENLEE
  Martha 51

GRIFFIN
  Owen 64

GRIGG, GRIGGS
  Anderson J. 77
  Jacob 46,47,52,66,70,76
  Jacob A. 25
  Joseph V. 45,52,58,77
  Joseph W. 49
  Moses 25,77
  Moses H. 25
  William 59,77

GUARLAND
  James D. 46

GUNTER
  George 40

GWINN
  John 46

HAGOOD
  Elizabeth 28
  Gregory 28,29,73
  Polly 28

HAIL, HAILE
  Benjamin 24
  Francis 43
  Jane 23,24

HAIRSTON
  Col. George 42,45
  Col. Samuel 42,45
  George 2,4,40,56
  Hardin 41,46,75
  Peter 75
  Robert 46
  Samuel 44

HALBERT
  John 29,46
  William 1

HALE
  Adam 58
  Benjamin 14
  Elizabeth 14
  John 14
  *Joseph 14
  Kezeiah 14
  Nancy 14
  Peter 14,63
  Rachel 14
  Thomas 14,63
  William 63
  Zachariah 64
  Zadock 58

HALL
  Adam 44,59,77
  Ann 32
  Delila 32
  Fleming 36,55,57
  Frankey 32
  Jeremiah 32
  Jonathan 32
  John 11,25,26,27,32,42,43,
    45,55,63,64,66,78
  John Sr. 40
  Molley 32
  Nancy 32
  Randal 32
  *Nathan 5,30,32,57,68
  Russell 32
  Sally 32
  Sarah 25,26
  Robert 12,13
  Thomas R. 25,32,42,45,65,67

HALL
  Thomas 32

HANAH
  William 8

HANBY
  David 29
  Gabriel 29,48,54,56,58
  James 29
  Jane 29
  *Jonathan 6,12,13,29,69
  John 29,63
  Mary 29
  Nancy 29
  Polly 29
  Peter 29
  Sally 29
  Samuel 29,44,45,47,68,69,
    70,71
  Samuel Jr 20, 52
  Sarah 77
  Susannah 29
  William 29,45,46,59,77

HANCOCK, HANDCOCK
  Abel 63
  Absalom 42,45
  Benjamin 9,22,61.62
  Gem 1
  *John 9,10,11
  John A. 62
  Lewis 9
  Major 9,25
  Susannah 9
  William 9,11,17,30,43,56,
    62,63

HAMMACKER, HAMMAKER
  John 58

HANDY
  Lucindy 34
  William 11

HANKS
  Drury 77

HANSBY
  Jemima 24
  John Sr. 24
  *Thomas 24

HARBOUR
  David 1,3,10,20,28,61,62
  John 41
  Joshua 3
  Keziah 3
  Moses 10, 28
  Naaman 28
  Nancy 3
  *Noah 30,70
  Mary 30
  Sara 3
  *Thomas 3,30,70

HARPER
  Hanah 25

HARRIS
  Barnard 44,46,66
  Benjamin James 16
  Bevin 32
  Betsy 32
  Claiborne 32,77
  Charlot 32
  Daniel 73
  Dicy 32
  Elijah 32,44,46,47,48,50,58
  Isham 43,63
  James 32,51
  Joel 30
  John 44,46
  Lydy 32
  Moses 30
  Nathan 63
  Obediah 66,75
  Patsey 32
  Polley 32
  Peggy 35
  Rebeccah 30
  Reuben 42,45,67
  Robert 32,58
  Salley 32
  Samuel 33,40,43,47,57,64
  *Sherad 32
  *William 30,35,40,64,74
  William Jr. 40,70
  Samuel Sr. 70

HARRISON
  Benjamin 38
  Col. Richard 73
  Francis 38,72
  Francis B. 73
  Francis P. 57
  George 38,59,73
  Polly 38
  *Richard 26,30,38,57,61,65,69,72,73
  Nicholas 38
  Susanah 26,38
  William 38

HART
  Cornelius 46

HARVEY
  Bash 74

HAWKINS
  Benjamin

HAWKS
  Abram 58
  John 58

HAYNES, HAINES
  *Bethany 19
  Hampton 60
  Joshua 19,58,68
  Lyles 19
  Morning 19
  Thomas 21
  William 19

HEATH
  Josiah 58
  William 74

HELTON, HILTON, HYLTON
  Edward 63
  Samuel 64

HENDERSON
  John 2,4

HENELEY
  Francis 63

HENSLEY
  Sukey 59

HERALD
  Jonathan 77

HERD
  Ann 27

HERRING
  Richard 45,48
  William 54

HICKERSON
  S. 57

HICKMAN
  Benjamin 42,45,64

HILL
  Charles 64
  Costilo 55,57
  John 77
  John P. 55
  Nancy 3
  Thomas 23,63,64

HINES, HINNES
  Benjamin 75
  Henry 58

HIX
  Farthing 48
  John 58, 77
  Lemuel 58

HODGE
  Abner

HOLLANDSWORTH
  Cornelius 23
  Daniel 59
  *Isaac 9,10,63
  James 23,63
  Mary 59
  Rebeccah 23
  Sarah 23
  Tandy 59
  Thomas 73

HOOKER
  John 64

HOPKINS
  Richard 34,41,47

HORNSBY
  Thomas 61

HORTON
  Jacob 58,77

HOUCHINS
  Bennet 10,17,43,63,67

HOUSTON
  Samuel 26

HOWARD
  Harry 72

HOWELL
  David 63
  Francis 55
  James 32,59,71
  Samuel 32,48,71

HUBBARD
  Benjamin 15,32,38,47,64
  Jesse 47
  Jonathan 47
  John 47
  Nancy 47
  Stephen 15,36,48,55

HUDSON
  Daniel 39
  David 39,45
  Hill 45
  *Jacob 39,45,58,69,78,79
  John B. 48
  John H. 39
  Obadiah 5,13
  Sally 39
  William R. 39

HUDSPETH
  Robert 12,13

HUDWELL
  Thomas 59

HUFF
  Mary 14

HUGHES
  Agnes 23
  *Archelaus 2,3,5,6,18
  Beverage 5
  *Beveridge 23
  Blackmore 23
  Francis 27
  John 6,12,20,23,24,34,39,
    41,46,51,56,57,75
  Leander 75
  Madison R. 75
  Mary 6,74
  M.R. 56
  Nancy 23
  Polly 23
  Reuben 56,74
  Sarah 23
  Samuel 39,41,76
  W.B. 62

HUNT
  Obadiah 60
  Thomas 50

HUNTER
  John 60

HURT
  Joseph 63
  Mary 37
  Moses 37

HUTCHESON-HUTCHERSON
  Arza 74
  Daniel 75
  Joseph 51
  Jeremiah 75

INGRAM -INGRUM
  Alexander 31,43,55,69
  Elizabeth 27
  James 8,27,31,43
  James Jr. 63,69
  James Sr. 69
  *James 31,55
  John 27,66
  John Sr. 27
  Martha 31,55,69

INGRAM - INGRUM cont'd
  Mary 31,55
  Paul C. 43,64
  Sarah 31

IRON
  John 59

ISBELL
  Thomas 24

JACKSON
  Joseph 25

JADWIN
  Jeremiah 4
  Soloman 4

JAMES
  John 14,40, 62,64
  Patsey 33
  Spencer 51,52

JARRETT
  Polly 34

JENNINGS
  Jonathan 77
  Robert 77
  William 75

JESSOP, JESSUP
  Elijah 58
  Joseph 25
  Joseph Sr. 58
  William 12

JOHNS
  Bartlett 64

JOHNSON
  Jane 46,71
  John 46,71
  Martin 46
  Mary 6
  Thomas 74

JOHNSTON
  John 70

JONES
  Ann 29
  Augustine 30
  Daniel 44
  Evon 77
  Ezekiel 60
  Edward 58
  Gabriel 29,30
  James 77
  Jesse 35,56,57,76
  John 30,33,78
  Levi 58
  Nancy 29,30
  Richard 51
  Sally 29,30,33
  *William 29,33,61,65,72
  Zilpha 29,30

JOYCE
  Alexander 53,74
  Andrew 14,44,62,65,66
  James 56,59
  John 59
  John Jr. 75
  Lucy R. 39
  Lydia 75
  Mary 19
  Lemuel 56,59
  Possom 75
  William 44
  William Jr. 56
  William Sr. 59
  William C. 59
  William T. 59

JUBALL & STRANGE 46

KALLAM
  David 51
  David Jr. 75
  David Sr. 75
  John 75

KEATON
  Clifton 53
  Cornelius 40
  Elizabeth 23
  James 40
  Mary 41
  Soloman 40,41,64
  William 1,40,41,46,59
  William Jr. 41
  Zackariah 1,23,41

KEATY
  Molly 23

KEETH
  James 30

KENNERLY
  Joseph 51,73

KENNON
  Samuel 5

KING
  John 74
  Robert 74
  *Samuel 3,7
  Tarleton 60
  Z. 75

++ below
KOGER, COGAR
  Henry 22,27,75
  Lucinda 39
  John 1,2,18,40,75
  John Jr. 22,27,55

LACKEY, LAKEY
  Alexander 14,17
  Esther 35
  George 18,40,41,62
  *John 1,4,18

LACY
  Theophilus 6,74

LADD
  Amos 11
  Thomas 11

LANDRITH
  Benjamin 24,45
  Benjamin B. 58
  Benjamin Jr. 24
  Benjamin R. 77
  Hannah 24
  Jonathan 27,45,59
  *McKindley 24,27
  Widow 58

++ KINGTON
  John 75

LANE, LAIN
  Edward 75
  George 10
  Rodue 9
  Samuel 11

LANKFORD
  West 59

LAMAN, LEAMAN
  George 46,71

LAW
  Chendle 60
  Robert 74,75

LAWRENCE
  Martin 23

LAWSON
  Jacob 12,13

LEAK, LEEK
  Andrew 34
  John 34
  Josiah 75
  Peter 51
  Peter F. 75

LEDBETTER
  Coleman 64

LEE
  Aaron 60
  George 26
  J.G. 57
  Joel 46
  Mary 33
  Richard 26
  William 44,56
  William Sr. 65

LENOX
  John 51

LESUER
  Grandason 36
  James 60

LEWIS
  Charles 46
  Charles Sr 71
  Edward 18,31,70

LINDSAY
  William 6

LITTRELL
  Rodham 12

LOCKHART
  Mary 22
  Robert 40,62,64

LUIS
  Alvern 63
  Edward 64

LOVE
  David 77

LOVING
  Dr. 54

LOW
  W. 56

LOWE
  Bird 40
  Robert 40

LOYD
  Robert 33

LYON
  Gincy 33
  *Humberston 1,4,5
  Jacob 33
  Jane 55
  James 5,53,77
  Nancy 5
  Stephen 1
  William 48, 57

MAC-MC
MC ALEXANDER
  Alexander 35
  Daniel 35
  David 35
  James 35
  John 35,42,45
  Isabelah 35
  Isabel 35
  Milly 35,76
  Rachel 35
  Tamer 35
  William 1,35,47

McALEXANDER cont'd
 *William Sr. 35,75

MC BRIDE
 Isaac 63
 James 43

McCAMPBELL
 James 16

McCLEERN
 Samuel 58

Mc CRAW
 Jacob 15
 Jacob A. 77
 James 58,77
 William 45,53,54,56,57,58,
    77
 William (Buck) 77
 William Jr. 58

Mc CUTCHEN
 Edith 36
 James 64
 William 64

McINTIRE
 Daniel 23,41,63

Mc KINNEY
 Stephen 58,77

McMILLAN, MCMILLION
 Dudley 58,77
 John N. 75
 Ruth 52
 William 27,45,52,77

McPEAK
 William 1,45

MANER see MAYNOR
 Stephen 63

MANKIN
 Esq. 59
 Jesse 46,47,58,68,70
 John 62,63,64

MANNING
 Mary 27
 Sarah 27
 *William 2

MAPES
 Joseph 63

MARROY
 Nicholas 45

MARSHALL
 John D. 73

MARTIN
 Andrew 51
 Baily 60
 Benjamin 8
 George 64
 Isaac 63,72
 James 77
 James, Jr 75
 Jiles 64
 John 15,51,54,77
 Joseph 56,59,74,75
 Richard 64
 Samuel 55,59,64,74,79
 William 55

MARTINDALE
 Daniel 46
 William 46

MASSEY
 Charles 60
 John 35,36,55,75
 Nancy 35,36
 Susanna 35,36
 W. 79
 Warren 42,43,45,55,56

MATLOCK
 John 74

MATTHEWS
 William 75

MAYNOR
 Ann 7
 Isaiah 7
 Jemimah 7
 Jeremiah 7
 John 7
 Joseph 60
 Pressiller 6
 *Richard Tucker 6,7,60
 Stephen 7
 Rody 7
 Tucker 6
 William 6

MAYO
  Benjamin 62,63
  Elizabeth 9
  Judith 9
  Polly 41
  Richardson 62
  Robert 41,66
  William James 10,11,17,63

MEDE
  Abel Jr. 63
  Jesse 63

MEDLEY
  John 60,63
  Samuel 63

MEEKS
  Martheu 1

MEELE
  Abrah. 63

MEREDEY
  Joseph 63,64

MICHEAUX 56

MILLER
  Joseph 64
  Martin 30,41,42,61

MILLS
  Richard 18,75,76
  William 75
  William J. 34

MITCHELL
  Daniel 48
  Thomas 6,63

MIZE
  Benjamin 63
  Frankey 27
  Isaac 64
  Ruth 27

MOLES
  James 10,40,64
  Jeremiah 64
  Jeremiah Jr. 64
  John 64
  Joseph 64

MOORE
  Alfred C. 47,50,52,53,54,5
  Claren 54
  Gallehue 47,52,53,54,56,57
    58,77
  Hardin H. 47,50,54,77
  Jane 58
  Jesse 37
  John 47,50,53,54,57,58
  Letha R. 48,50,53,54,58
  Mary 37
  Madison T. 47,48,50,54,58
  Patience Jane 48,50,54,56
  Rhode 15
  Reuben 75
  Samuel 47,48,50,53,54,57,
    58,77
  William 42,44,45,47,50,
    51,54,58,59,65,76,77
  William H. 48,54,58

MORAN
  James 75

MORGAN
  Con... 18
  David 2,4
  Gardner P. 18

MORRIS
  Benjamin 34
  Jane 35
  John 34
  Samuel C. 34
  *Samuel C. 34
  Susanna 34
  Thomas J. 34
  William 34,74

MORRISON
  Allen 9
  James 23
  Jincy 9
  Mary 9
  Nathaniel 63

MORROW, MORREY
  Matthew 11,63
  Thomas 1,4

MOSS
  Elizabeth 42,45
  Mary Ann 26

MULLINS
  Booker 60

MURPHY
  James 65
  Jesse 46,73

MURRAY
  Nicholas 59

NANCE
  Anne 28
  Edmund 29
  Elender 28
  Euritit 35

NASH
  Benjamin 43
  Claburn 63

NELSON
  Ann 37
  Tap 74
  William 59

NEW
  Mary 40

NEWBERRY
  William 42,45

NEWMAN
  Joseph 65,67

NOE
  Aaron 60
  Adam 60

NOLEN,NOWLIN,NOWLAND
  David 31
  Francis 53
  *James 4,31,69
  Richard 40,43,64
  Samuel 31,48
  Ursula 31
  William Jr. 58

NORTON
  James 77
  John 15

NUNNS
  John 8,24

OLDHAM
  Thomas 63

ONEAL
  John 45

OWEN, OWENS
  *Elizabeth 9
  Hannah 27
  James 46
  John 64
  Leonard 9,58,77

PACE
  John 51

PACKWOOD
  Elisha 36,71
  Elizabeth 36
  Judith 33
  Larkin 36
  Nancy 36
  *Samuel 28,36,71
  Richard 36
  William 36

PARKER
  John 59
  Rachel 14

PARMER
  David 37,63
  Edward 37,57,63
  Elizabeth 37
  John 37
  Malachi 37,40,62,64
  Mary 37
  Sally 37
  Samuel 37
  Susannah 37
  *William 37
  William Sr. 23

PARR
  Ann 20,21
  Arthur 1,24
  Cindy M. 20,21,32
  Greensville 24
  *Henry 1,13

PARR cont'd
 *John,Jr 1,5,13,20,24,61
 John Sr 1,62
 *John 1,24,44
 John Edm. 32
 John E. 21,44
 Isham 20,21
 Mark 20,21,61
 Mary 1,20,21,33,46,56
 Mazy 13
 Milly 1
 Miriam 24
 Nancy 13,32,44,55
 Noah 24,41
 Sarah 20,21
 c Smith 20,32
 Thanny 44
 Thomas 13,20,21
 William 20,32

PARSONS
 William 63

PART
 John 4

PAYNE
 John 60

PEAKE
 W. 44

PEARCE
 David 58,59

PELPHREY
 James 63

PENDLETON
 Prior 30,47

PENN
 Abram 56,68
 *Abraham 8,10,20
 Capt.Gabriel 41
 Clark 53
 Col. G. 73
 Edmund 20
 Gabriel 6,8,9,20,24,42,44,
  46,61,64,68,71,74,78
 George 8,9,16,20,24,26,30,
  34,38,41,42
 Green 64
 Greensville 18,28,38,51,
  74,75,78
 George, Sr. 34
 Horatio 34,46

PENN cont'd
 James 34,44,75
 *Phillip 20
 Reaha 64
 Ruth 8
 T.J. 78
 Thomas 26,40,41,51,64,
  65,78
 William 40

PENNINGTON
 Isaac 13
 Mildred 63
 Robert 63

PERDEY see PURDY

PEREGOY
 Abel 63

PERKINS
 David 26,41,42
 Christian 26,42
 Elizabeth 26,42
 Suky 26
 Susannah 42,45
 Thomas 26,42,45
 *William 26,42,45,65

PERKINS & WALKER 53

PHILLIPS
 Henry 74
 John 75

PHILPOTT
 Ben 58
 Benjamin 63
 Edward 7,55,72,73
 John 7,58
 John W. 60
 Lucy 30
 Samuel 7

PIERCE
 David 59

PIGG
 George 25,63

PIKE
 Isaac 77
 Joseph 58

PILSON
  Esther 17
  Richard 1,40
  Tobe 63
  William 17,43,63

POINDEXTER
  John 56

POOR
  Hugh 59
  Stephen 59

POTEET
  John 18

POWERS
  John 75

PRATER
  Nehemiah 77

PRICE
  Barnard More 3,7,41,56
  William (dec'd) 63

PRILLAMAN
  Elizabeth 36
  George 60
  Jacob 31,60

PUCKETT
  Isham 58,77
  James 77
  John 59

PURDY -PERDEY
  John 63
  Zekel 63

QUARLES
  Abraham 16
  James 16
  Judith 16

RADFORD
  Jesse 59

RAGAN
  John 75

RAKES
  Charles 43,45,63
  Chesley 78
  Elisha 45,64
  John 42

RANDLEMAN
  Dr. 1

RATLIFF
  Elizabeth 25
  Fanny 25
  John 25
  Mary 25
  Pheby 25
  Silas 25
  *Silus, Sr. 25
  Usley 25

RAY
  Benjamin 24

REA
  Aaron 13
  David 34,75
  Horsley 34
  *John 5,34,39,66,75,76
  Joseph 34
  Mildred 34

REDLEY
  John 74,75

REDMAN
  Caty 38
  John 38,74

REED
  John 74
  Michael 75

REEVES, REAVES
  George 6
  John 40,63
  Josiah 40,63
  Thomas 22,41,61,62,63,64

REMSEY
  Benjamin 64

REYNOLDS
  Abraham 41
  Bartlet 64
  Bengan 77
  Benjamin 58
  James 10
  Johnson 58
  Joseph 26,40,42,45,64
  Milly 22
  Nathaniel 58
  Richard 63
  Sarah 26,42

REYNOLDS cont'd
  Thomas 70,72
  William 58,77
  William Sr. 58

RICHARDSON
  John a. Sr. 77

RICKMAN
  John 53

RIGG
  Townley 40,41,64

ROBERTS
  Shadrack 59

ROBERTSON
  Benjamin Skinner 22
  David 43,47,67
  David Jr. 38,43
  Elizabeth 22
  Genea 22
  George 21
  John 77
  *Milly 38,43,47
  Nancy 21,22
  Rebecca 22
  Sally 22,43
  *William 21,22

ROBSON
  Eggans 1

ROGERS
  Ann 33,36,37
  *Clement 36,78
  David 4,37
  George 44,46
  Hyder A. 75
  John S. 37
  Josiah 53
  Robert 66
  Sarah S. 37

ROSS
  David 63
  Job 5
  Lewis 62
  Nancy 31
  Nathaniel 16,64
  William 63

ROWAN
  Betsy 17
  Robert 8,17,20,43

ROWARK
  Elijah 15

ROWLAND
  Washington 43

RUSK
  *John 26
  Nelly 26,27
  Sally 26

RYAN
  William 63

SALSBERRY
  Elizabeth 63
  William 11,63,64

SAMMONS
  *Peter 13

SAMPSON
  Vernon 77

SANDEFER
  M. 42,44,46,52,55,57,61,
    65,70,71,72,74,75
  Mathew 31,33,34,36,48

SAUNDERS
  Caty 31
  Col. Peter 43
  Joel 11
  Joseph 11
  Peter 4,18,43
  Samuel 42,45,55,57,59

SAWYERS
  William 44,58

SCALES
  John 51,75
  Joseph 74
  Nathaniel 51,58,74,75
  Oney 51
  Peter 6,51,74,76
  Pleasant 51,74
  P.D. 51,74
  Randal D. 51

SCOTT
  John 9,59
  Robert 17

SHAFFER
  John 75

SHARP
  John 12
  John Jr. 40,41
  John Sr. 64
  Joseph 46
  Matilda 28
  Philpenia 48
  Samuel 1
  Richard 40,63,64
  Thomas 60
  William 46,48,63
  William Jr. 40
  William Sr. 40

SHEELOR, SHEALOR
  Anne 33
  Daniel 43
  Jacob 57

SHELTON
  Abstam 37
  Claiborne 18,48
  Eliphaz 12,18
  Hezekiah 5
  James 1
  John 30,73
  Palatiah 1
  William 30
  Winnefred 29,30

SHIVAL
  Benjamin 74

SHIVELY
  John 42,45

SHOCKLEY
  James 77

SHORT
  Reuben 43,55,63

SIMMONS
  Jesse 75
  William 75

SIMMS
  Exoney 28
  *Ignatious 28,59,60,72
  Ignatious Andrew Jackson
    28,29
  Jannet 28,29
  John 60
  John Dabney 28,29
  Marget 28
  Marmaduke Manor 29
  William Robertson 28,29

SIMON
  David P. 45

SLADE
  William 53,57

SLUAGHTER
  Dandridge 10,11,37,57
  John 72

SMALL
  Beky 1
  *John 1,4
  Malen 1
  Matthew 1,4
  Mary 1

SMALLMAN
  *John 6

SMITH
  Augustine H. 31
  Bartlett 8,44,45,50,58,77
  Bartholomew 32,44,55,56,77
  Burwell 49,59
  Charles 36
  H. 2,6
  Henry 5,55,32
  Humphrey 5,18
  Harbart 13,55,32
  Hannah 33,79
  George 45,58
  Isham,Isaam 32,55,56
  Joseph 13,44,45,52,57,59,
    73,76,77
  John 21,22,24,27,32,33,
    44,46,56,59,68,37,53,69
  James 44,77
  Jackson 46
  Lucy 22
  *Meredith 22

SMITH cont'd
  Mary 22
  Munford 27,32,44,48,50,53,
    58,68,69,73,77,79
  Mallory 50
  Mark 55
  Nathaniel 5,12,14,20,32,
    42,44,46,55,56,61,62,66,
    67,68
  Peter 29,36,51,60
  Rachel 36
  Samuel 58,60
  Susannah 44,55
  Thomas 52,75
  William Jr. 5,21,46,56,69
  *William Sr. 5,32,44,53,55,
    56,69
  William 14,44,58,68,33,44,
    46,56,59,68
  Williamson 46,53,56

SMOTHERS
  Thomas 64

SNEED
  Abraham 33
  James 33
  John 22,33,43,67,68
  *John Sr. 33
  Nancy 33
  Richard 33
  Samuel 33
  Thomas 55,63
  William 25,33,43,62,68

SNOW
  Hale 58,77
  Ice 59
  Johnson 45,77
  Richard 58
  Thomas 58,77

SNYDER
  W.V. 74

SPALDEN, SPAULDEN, SPADING
  Francis 63,64
  John 42,45,64
  John 42,45,64,68
  Thomas 64

SPEARS
  James 24

SPENCER
  John 40
  Mary 30,37
  Sarah 37
  Thomas 63
  William 60

SPRAGER
  John 58
  John W. 59

SPROUSE
  George 41

SPURLOCK
  James 1
  Jesse 3

STANLEY, STANDLEY
  C. 44
  Christopher 46,53,75
  John 59
  Sindy 55
  Thomas 55
  William 60

STAPLES
  A. 58,76
  Abram 48
  Edward 41
  Edward C. 51,75
  George S. 74
  John 75
  Mary S. 41
  S. 48
  Samuel 8,16,18,20,22,23,
    2,44,46,57,58

STEEL
  William 15,75

STEPHENS
  Martha 59

STEVENS
  Phillip 63
  Soloman 64

STEWART
  James 15

STOE
  *Garrett 12

STOKES
  Fanney 26
  Richard 26

STONE
  Daneil 51
  Elizabeth 60
  Esibeah 60
  Eusebus 29,72
  Jeremiah 63
  John 60
  Martha 60
  Micajah 29,60
  Patsy 60
  Richard 36,60
  Stephen 60
  Tandy 60
  William 29,64

STOVALL
  Brett 6,8,16,21,26,41,
    42,49,56,57,59,64
  Dr. L.P. 51
  Joseph 8,9,18,30,61

STOVER
  Jacob 64
  Obediah 63

STRANGE
  John 61
  Robert 44

STURDHOUSE
  Betsey 23

STUART
  Arch. 57,59

SUMMERS
  Caleb 15

SUTTON
  Charles 3

SUTFIN
  William 77

SWITZER
  JOhn 74

TALLEY
  Spencer 4

TALIFERRO
  L. M. 73

TATE
  James 58
  Jarrel 59

TATUM
  Capt. John 53
  Cash 46
  Edward 5,8,12,15
  J. 71,76,50
  Jesse 61
  John 29,39,40,44,45,46,
    52,58,59,65,67,68,69
  Landall 21

TAYLOR
  Elizabeth 74
  *James 5,10,22,40,44,65,
  David 22,30,62,63,64,
    69,75
  James Jr. 63
  Jefferson 55,57
  Nancy 40
  Reuben 40

TENNISON
  Thomas 43,55,64,68
  Zalphiniah 64,66,70

TERRY
  Benjamin 47,48,72
  John 48
  Nancy 47,48,72
  Polly 48
  Robert 54
  Sally 48
  Samuel 48
  Viney 47,48,72

THOMAS
  Allen 74
  *Augustine 38,41,39,75
  Augustine Bartholomew 39
  Benjamin 39
  Capt. Richard 33

THOMAS cont'd
  Charles 2
  Charles Jr. 27,42,43,45,68
  Charles Sr. 65,67
  Cornelius 63
  Dibby 3
  Deborah 39
  Edward 39,56
  James Jr. 63
  James Waring 39
  Mary 39
  Pleasant 45
  R. 56
  Rachel 39
  Richard 17,43,46,55,64,68,
      74,78
  Washington 38

THOMPSON, THOMSON
  Elizabeth 23
  Francis 63
  Henry 30
  Jesse 44
  John 77
  Mary 9,31
  William 18,30,40,44,64

TIFTON
  William 58

TILLY
  Edward 51,59

TINSLEY
  Jane 26

TITTLE
  Lydda 23
  Sally 14

TRAYLOR
  John C. 51,58

TRENT
  *Alexander 12
  Elijah 75

TUCKER
  *Frances 26
  George 74
  Nancy 26
  Robert 26

TUGGLE
  James 33,57
  *John 33,35,56,64
  John Jr. 35
  John Sr. 56,74
  Henry 33,57
  Nancy 33

TUNE
  Thomas 54

TURMAN, TERMAN
  Benjamin 3
  John 64

TURNER
  Adam 10,15,17,40,42,43,45,
      56,63,65,67,74
  Elizabeth 40,43
  Ellenor 13
  *Francis 1,17,40,43
  G.W. 52
  James 8,15,17,40,43,60,62
  John 15,17,20,23,40,43,
      62,70
  John Sr. 62
  Josiah 7
  Judith 38
  Lewis 59
  Meshack 60
  Obediah 60
  William 60

UNTHANK
  Jonathan 53

VANCEL, VANNIEL
  Adam 31
  Caty 31
  Edmond 31,44
  Elias 31,44,45
  Isaac 31
  John 31,44
  *John 31,44,45
  John Jr. 44
  Jonas 31,44
  Mary 31
  Samuel 31,44
  Tobias 31

VAUN
  Richard 63

VAWTER, VAUGHTER
    Clement 46,71

VERNON
    Mary 75
    Wilson S. 75

VIA, VIER
    James 57,74
    Sarah 63
    William 18,42,45,56,60,69

WALDEN
    Margarett 27
    Moses 7
    William 27,64,66

WALKER
    D. 57
    Dabney 52,77
    John 75
    John B. 59
    Martin 58
    Samuel 77
    William 74

WARD
    Thomas 2

WASHINGTON
    George 55,78

WATKINS
    Ebenzer 42,45

WATS
    Reuben 46

WEBB
    Ann 4
    Elizabeth 40
    Floyed 46,53
    *Isam 4
    John 13,44,45,46,77
    S.R. 77
    Susannah 21
    William 4

WEBSTER
    Richard 75

WEDDLE
    John 31,44

WELLS
    Richard 57

WHALEN
    James 11

WHALEY, WHALING
    James 63
    John 63
    Richard 63
    Rhody 63

WHITLOCK
    John 50,53,58
    Richard L. 56
    Thomas 46,52,57,66,70,
        73,76,77

WILKS
    Francis 41,45

WILLIAMS
    Edward Parker 56
    Elizabeth 50,59
    Jesse 12,25
    Phillip 42,45
    William 8,77

WILLIS
    Greensville 58
    Joseph Jr. 5
    Thomas 64
    William 64

WILSON
    Charles 46
    John 13
    Obediah 46
    Robert 45

WITT, WHIT
    Arch. 44
    Daniel 48,74,75
    William 16,18
    William Sr. 63

WOOD, WOODS
    Fanny 55
    Jeremiah 53
    John 74

WOOTEN
    Constable 51
    John 60
    Thomas J. 75

WRAY
  William 60

WRIGHT
  Elizabeth 25
  Fanny 25
  John 25
  Josiah 25
  Mary 25
  Reuben 25
  Sarah 43
 *Robert 25,43,62,64

YOUNG
  James 59
  Jesse 51,59
  Peter 60
  Nathaniel C. 59
  Sarah 59

www.ingramcontent.com/pod-product-compliance
Lightning Source LLC
Chambersburg PA
CBHW020659300426
44112CB00007B/444